Understanding ADHD

Future Books is an imprint of Future Publishing Limited, Quay House, The Ambury, Bath, BA1 1UA

A catalogue record for this book is available from the British Library.

ISBN 978-1-83648-927-6 hardback

The paper holds full FSC certification and accreditation.

Printed in China, for Future Publishing Limited

GPSR EU RP (for authorities only)
eucomply OÜ Pärnu mnt 139b-14 11317
Tallinn, Estonia
hello@eucompliancepartner.com
+3375690241

Interested in Foreign Rights to publish this title? Email us at:
licensing@futurenet.com

Group Editor
Philippa Grafton

Contributors
Edoardo Albert, Julie Bassett, Dr Sinead Doyle, Ben Grafton, Emma Green, Natalia Lubomirski, Julia Mitchell, Alice Pattillo

Senior Art Editor
Andy Downes

Head of Art & Design
Greg Whitaker

Editorial Director
Jon White

Managing Director
Grainne McKenna

Production Project Manager
Matthew Eglinton

Global Business Development Manager
Jennifer Smith

Head of Future International & Bookazines
Tim Mathers

Cover images
Adobe Stock

FUTURE Connectors. Creators. Experience Makers.

Future plc is a public company quoted on the London Stock Exchange (symbol: FUTR)
www.futureplc.com

Chief Executive Officer **Kevin Li Ying**
Non-Executive Chairman **Mark Brooker**
Chief Financial Officer **Sharjeel Suleman**

Tel +44 (0)1225 442 244

FSC www.fsc.org MIX Paper | Supporting responsible forestry FSC® C008047

Understanding ADHD

If you, or anyone you know, is affected by ADHD, the following charities and helplines are ready to offer free support:

UK

ADHD UK - **adhduk.co.uk**
UK Adult ADHD Network - **ukaan.org**

USA

Children and Adults with Attention-Deficit/Hyperactivity Disorder (CHADD) - **chadd.org**
Attention Deficit Disorder Association - **add.org**
American Professional Society of ADHD and Related Disorders (APSARD) - **apsard.org**

Australia

The ADHD Foundation - **adhdfoundation.org.au**
ADHD Support Australia - **adhdsupportaustralia.com.au**
ADDults with ADHD - **adultadhd.org.au**

Disclaimer

This publication is for information only and is not intended to substitute professional medical advice and should not be relied on as health or personal advice. Never disregard professional advice or delay seeking it.

Always consult your pharmacist or GP for guidance before using any natural, holistic, over-the-counter or prescription remedies, and read any instructions carefully. In an emergency, call the emergency services and seek professional help immediately. Readers rely on any information at their sole risk, and Understanding ADHD, and its publisher, Future Publishing Ltd, limit their liability to the fullest extent permitted by law.

Welcome

As diagnoses of ADHD soar and waiting lists for referrals stretch on for years, it can seem increasingly difficult to find support and an explanation for why you are the way that you are. In this brand new title, we'll explore what exactly ADHD is and how it can impact your life, from infancy all the way through to adulthood.

Whether you were termed a troublemaker at school because you couldn't concentrate in class, or you've found yourself chronically overthinking relationships or experiencing executive dysfunction as a grown-up, it can be reassuring to know that you're not alone. It's estimated that around 22 million adults in the US have ADHD, while in the UK that's around 2.6 million people, but less than a quarter of these have an official diagnosis. We'll guide you through what ADHD is and how it might be affecting you, and we'll share some expert-approved ways to manage your symptoms, from how to beat imposter syndrome and thrive at work, to how to support your child if you suspect they're living with ADHD.

Contents

10 What is neurodiversity?
How different ways of thinking gives rise to new ways of seeing and experiencing the world

16 Understanding ADHD
Complex yet common, ADHD gives individuals unique strengths and challenges

22 Women and hormones
How the menstrual cycle and menopause affect women who live with ADHD

26 Seeking a diagnosis
We walk you through the process of getting diagnosed

30 Is ADHD overdiagnosed?
A rise in diagnoses might not be telling the full story

32 ADHD in adulthood
We've spoken to two people who received an ADHD diagnosis as adults

42 Treatments and coping mechanisms
There are many ways to manage ADHD, from medication to therapy and self-help

48 Comorbidities
How other conditions present with ADHD, including other neurodiversities, as well as anxiety and depression

52 Mental health masterclass
Feeling different can be hard, and mental wellbeing can suffer

58 Grounding techniques
Self-soothing routines that you can do to stop your anxiety spiralling out of control

66 What is masking?
We explain what the concept of 'masking' is, and what the effects of it can be

70 Does my child have ADHD?
How does ADHD manifest itself in children, and is it something to worry about?

76 Supporting your child
Failing to recognise ADHD can cause children to struggle academically and socially

84 Sticks and stones
We're aware of the impact bullying has on kids, but ignore scarred adults left in its wake

90 The emotional rollercoaster
Emotional dysregulation is rife among those living with ADHD

98 Feeling inferior
Neurodiverse people may struggle with self-esteem. Why is that, and how can you heal?

102 Executive dysfunction
We explore what executive function is, and how it can be impacted in those with ADHD

110 Feeling overwhelmed
Why do those with ADHD experience overwhelm, and how can you handle it?

116 A matter of interest
The interest-based nervous system helps us understand attention and motivation

124 Improve memory and concentration
Tips and tricks to boost your working memory and focus

128 How to avoid seeing red
Learn how to master your anger response and diffuse difficult situations

134 The 'F' word
When friends seem few and far between, ADHD may be playing havoc with your social life

140 Narcissists and the neurodiverse
We explore why those with ADHD risk falling into a cycle of toxic and abusive partnerships

144 ADHD in the workplace
Embracing your ADHD can lead to a fulfilling work life

What is neurodiversity?

How different ways of thinking gives rise to new ways of seeing and experiencing the world

Words Edoardo Albert

Some people are tall, others short. There are people with blue eyes, brown eyes, grey eyes, green eyes and a few even have different colour eyes. The writer of this feature has UK size ten feet; yours are probably another size. The simple fact is that people are different. It's so unremarkable that we do not even notice it. The only time this difference does become noticeable is when we meet people who are not different: identical twins stand out from the rest of the population precisely because they look just like another person, not because they look different.

People are strange

It is the fact of difference across a range that unifies us. If you mapped out the heights of everybody alive in the world today, it would form what is known as a bell curve. That's the sort of curve that looks like,

> **"There are significant sub-sections of the population who think differently"**

well, a bell: a long slow rise, then a sudden acceleration up to the top of the curve and a smooth turn down before another long, slow decline at the other end. What that means is that the vast majority of people are a few inches either side of the average height, with far fewer at the extremes. There are billions of people between 1.5 and 1.8 metres (five and six feet) in height, but only about 2,400 people who are over 2.1 metres (seven feet).

But while this might be obvious so far as our outsides are concerned, for some reason we tend not to apply that to what goes on inside, in our minds. There, we have a strong tendency to think that what applies to us applies to everyone. The most obvious example comes at the level of our basic self-awareness, the space inside our minds where we and the world meet. People assume that everyone else experiences consciousness in the same way they do. But that's not how it is. The most common way of thinking is through an inner voice: literally words in one's mind. These can be monologues, dialogues or even multi-part plays with lots of different voices shouting at each other. However, some people think visually, conjuring up images. Others think emotionally, or with their senses. A few even think non-symbolically (which is something only other people who think like this truly understand).

Different strokes for different folks

This is the core of neurodiversity. It's the psychological equivalent of the height distribution of the general population. Most people think along roughly the same lines but there are significant sub-sections of the population who think differently. In most cases, these differences are part of a continuum. Those people who are neurodiverse simply lie further out along the curves than the majority of the population. In some ways, these differences can be a strength. A taller than average person can reach up and get something from the top shelf that a person of average height can't reach - or even play professional basketball. An autistic person's eye for detail may lead them to spot an error in coding that's stopping a computer program from working.

However, it's also true that the extremes of any trait - physical or mental - can produce difficulties. The world's tallest person in recorded history, Robert Wadlow, died at the age of 22 because his heart could not cope with the size of his body, and the same is true of almost all the other extremely tall people in history. Wadlow suffered from gigantism, where his body never stopped growing. Autism is similarly listed as a developmental disorder. However, in most cases, while challenging, it's not crippling. Having said that, for people who never develop language as the result of autism, it obviously makes life extremely difficult for them and their carers. This does not render such people subhuman nor does it make their lives worthless, but it does make their lives more difficult.

Neurodiverse or mentally ill?

A paranoid schizophrenic who hears voices telling them to kill their child's teacher definitely sees the world differently from most people, and their mind works differently too. So by a simple definition of neurodivergence, paranoid schizophrenics are neurodivergent. The same could be said of people suffering from clinical depression, bipolar disorder and other severe mental-health conditions.

In one sense, this is true. Everyone suffering from severe mental illness is neurodivergent - if they weren't, then the majority of the population would be mentally ill. However, in the case of mental illness, the neurological difference can be devastating to the life of the sufferer and the people around them. A good example is the different ways people with autism and OCD experience routines. An autistic person, particularly a child, will use routines to help control situations, thus reducing anxiety and helping them feel better. For instance, one of the writer's sons had a five-minute goodbye routine that he had to go through every morning before entering school. His teachers initially found this annoying but allowing him to complete the routine enabled him to calm down and face the day better. This is very different to how a person with OCD experiences routines. In that case, they run through their routines despite the fact that they make them feel worse - they can't stop themselves from doing so. So mental illness begins where life starts going downhill.

From normal to neurodiverse

The term 'neurodiversity' was first proposed in the 1990s by Judy Singer, an Australian sociologist. The 1990s was also when the internet was developed and its existence enabled neurodiverse people around the world to connect with each other. Suddenly, they and their families and friends realised that they were not oddballs, freaks or weirdos (terms many were all too familiar with) but rather people whose minds simply worked differently from the norm, with their own strengths and weaknesses.

With this recognition, a movement to advocate for the rights of neurodiverse people developed.

Originally, it focused most on people with autism and ADHD but latterly it has broadened so that it includes anyone who thinks differently from the norm and whose life is impacted by this. As psychologists have examined the workings of the human mind more closely, and people have felt more empowered to speak out, more and more differences in the way people think have come to the fore. These include conditions that are a result of differences in development, such as autism and dyspraxia, as well as acquired conditions, such as dementia and PTSD.

Difference and difficulty

While neurodivergent people gain insights and fresh perspectives on problems that the rest of us may struggle with, it's nonetheless clear that living with neurodivergence is not all plain sailing through a neurotypical sea.

Some of these difficulties are a result of the neurodivergence itself - a strength in one area usually entails a weakness in another. For instance, someone with dyspraxia might love music but will find it very difficult to become a concert pianist. That's a problem inherent to the dyspraxia.

But on the other hand, there are the difficulties that are imposed from without. These are the result of the wider society not understanding or appreciating people with neurodiversity. For instance, a dyspraxic adult may be an excellent worker but they might require longer to type up a report. This difficulty could be resolved by allowing them to dictate the report rather than typing it - a small accommodation that could have big results.

Generally speaking, neurodiverse people simply want to have a chance to make their own unique

Made this way

The term neurodivergence was first used by people with autism. It was then quickly adopted by people with ADHD, dyspraxia, dyscalculia and dyslexia. Medically, these are labelled as developmental disorders since they first manifest themselves in childhood. Recent research, particularly on autism, has started us towards understanding what happens. As the brain develops, billions of new connections between neurones are made as the baby learns to move, talk and walk. The brain is literally wiring itself up for future life. But in doing so it creates millions of unnecessary connections. Between the ages of two and ten, this process goes into reverse and the developing brain starts pruning synaptic connections. Developmental disorders such as autism appear to be a result of the brain pruning less in some areas than normal. For instance, the sensory sensitivities experienced by many autistic people are probably the result of a lack of pruning in the sensory pathways of the brain. So while not necessarily born neurodivergent, their brains become different early in life.

However, the idea of neurodivergence has widened in recent years to include people whose brains change in later life. This can include the physical changes associated with dementia and the psychological changes produced by conditions such as PTSD. So now, neurodivergence is something that can apply both to people born different and to people who become different.

contribution to society. To do so, they might need the rest of us to change how we do some things. These are generally small alterations but making them will enable the rest of us to benefit from the unique ways of seeing and doing things that neurodivergent people can bring to the table.

After all, if everyone is looking at a problem in the same way, then they will all focus on the same solutions. It takes someone seeing the problem in a new way to come up with a fresh solution. So welcoming and accommodating neurodiverse people within society will make us all stronger.

Understanding ADHD

A complex yet commonly experienced disorder, Attention Deficit Hyperactivity Disorder (ADHD) gives individuals a unique combination of strengths and difficulties

Words Julia Mitchell

A common form of neurodiversity, ADHD is a condition that usually begins in childhood and lasts for someone's entire life. Although it can cause a variety of difficulties in everyday functioning for both children and adults, people with ADHD also have many strengths that make them fantastic family members, friends and employees. It's likely that you know someone who has ADHD – it's estimated that three to four per cent of adults in the UK live with the condition, with around five per cent of children meeting the diagnostic criteria globally. Recent years have seen increased awareness about ADHD, predominantly due to social media, which has led to an increase in individuals seeking a diagnosis.

What are the different types of ADHD?

ADHD is an umbrella term that can be broken down into three main subtypes: hyperactive/impulsive, inattentive, and combined. The idea behind this is that people generally present with different symptoms depending on the subtype, and are then diagnosed accordingly. For example, an individual with predominantly inattentive ADHD might experience difficulties following instructions and concentrating in class. This subtype is also known as ADD, although the term is now less frequently used. Other people with predominantly hyperactive/impulsive ADHD might find themselves interrupting others during conversations and find it difficult to sit still, while people diagnosed with combined type ADHD will possess a combination of the two sets of symptoms. Although thinking about ADHD in this way can help people to gain a stronger understanding of how they see and interact with the world, it's important to remember that this is a rough guide, and a person's symptoms will often not fit neatly into one box.

What causes ADHD?

Although it's not known exactly what causes ADHD, it's thought that a number of factors may be involved. The first of these is genetics, and research has found that ADHD often runs in families. This means that children who have relatives with ADHD are four times more likely to also have the condition. Other groups that are found to be at an increased risk of developing ADHD include people with traumatic brain injuries and epilepsy, as well as those who were born prematurely or at a low birthweight. It's thought that essential brain development occurs in the later stages of pregnancy, and babies that are born significantly early miss out on this brain development happening before birth.

Other research has identified changes in the brains of people with ADHD. For example, a part of the brain called the prefrontal cortex – which helps with emotional control, time management, organisation and problem-solving – is often smaller in children with the condition. Brain chemicals known as neurotransmitters also vary in those with ADHD, and this includes lower levels of the pleasure chemical dopamine, which is involved in the brain's reward system. While experts have much to learn about the causes of ADHD, research is ongoing, meaning that we might one day have a clearer picture about how it develops.

Common symptoms of ADHD

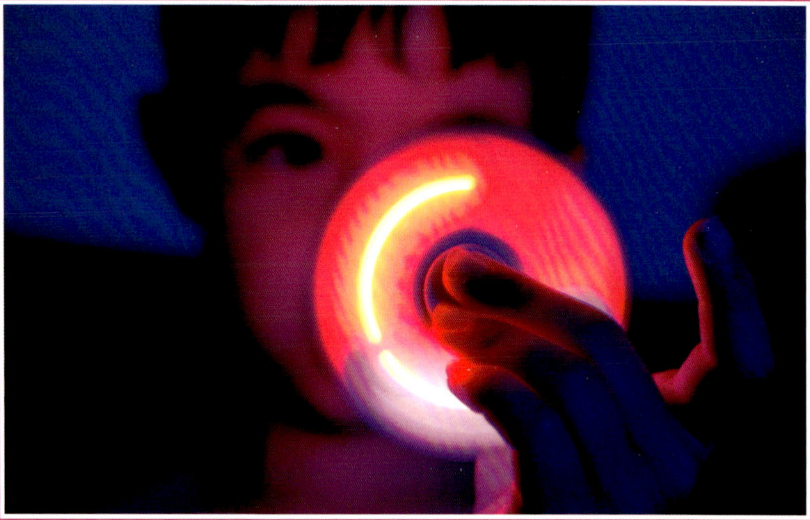

A broad condition with three subtypes, there are many different symptoms that are associated with ADHD. Each person's experience with the condition is unique, and it's not uncommon for people to experience different combinations of symptoms.

According to the UK's National Health Service (NHS), the criteria for children and teenagers with ADHD is well defined and agreed upon by experts. The symptoms of inattentiveness ADHD often include having a short attention span, being easily distracted, as well as making careless mistakes, for example, in schoolwork. Children with this type of ADHD might also seem forgetful, constantly be losing things, or have difficulties completing tasks that are tedious or time-consuming. Other potential symptoms of inattentiveness include seeming unable to listen to or carry out instructions, constantly changing activity or having difficulty organising tasks.

Symptoms of hyperactivity and impulsivity often present a bit differently, and can include being unable to sit still, especially in calm or quiet surroundings, fidgeting a lot and being unable to concentrate on tasks. Some children may seem to talk or move excessively, have difficulties waiting their turn, act without thinking, interrupt conversations, or have little or no sense of danger.

Adults can experience similar symptoms, as well as different ones. These can include carelessness and a lack of attention to detail, continually starting new tasks before finishing old ones, poor organisational skills and the inability to focus or prioritise. Other symptoms can include continually losing or misplacing things, forgetfulness, restlessness, difficulty keeping quiet, and speaking out of turn. Some people might find that they blurt out responses and interrupt others, experience mood swings, easily become irritable and have a quick temper, have an inability to deal with stress, exhibit extreme impatience and frequently take risks that might be dangerous or unsafe.

Gender differences

While it was previously believed that ADHD was more likely to occur in boys rather than girls, our understanding has progressed greatly over the years, and we now know that it commonly presents in all genders, although the symptoms can vary. For example, girls and women are more likely to experience symptoms that present internally. This can include feelings of being overwhelmed, a lack of motivation, being disorganised and feeling forgetful, shyness due to social anxiety, and perfectionism. Boys and men, on the other hand, are more likely to experience external behaviours that are more obvious to other people. This can include seeming disruptive and aggressive, outbursts of anger and general insensitivity. Although these are patterns that have been observed by experts, these differences should be considered as more of a guide rather than a set of rules, and they won't necessarily apply to everyone.

> **"Each person's experience with ADHD is unique, and may face a different combination of symptoms"**

What difficulties can people with ADHD have?

People with ADHD can experience a variety of difficulties depending on their symptoms, particularly if they are undiagnosed and don't know why they behave like they do. With children and young people this can manifest through difficulties at school, causing behaviour that may be disruptive as they struggle to concentrate and contain impulsive actions. Whether at home or at school, symptoms like these can be challenging, but they are not the child or young person's fault, and

there are many ways that they can be supported. Symptoms in adults tend to be more subtle in nature - this is often because individuals have learned how to manage or mask their symptoms.

It's common for people with ADHD to experience rejection sensitive dysphoria (known as RSD), which can make relationships with others challenging. RSD is an intense emotional reaction that occurs in response to feeling rejected by others. It doesn't matter whether they have actually been rejected or not, the strong emotions that accompany RSD are very real and can be difficult to manage. This can impact on how individuals interact with others, and can sometimes result in being misdiagnosed with social anxiety caused by their attempts to avoid feelings of RSD.

On a practical level, people with ADHD can also commonly experience difficulties at work or with keeping on top of things at home. Known as executive dysfunction, it can be difficult for individuals with ADHD to organise themselves, manage their time and prioritise tasks. It can also be more challenging for them to initiate tasks, finding themselves in a state of task paralysis that either delays or completely stops them from getting things done. It's very easy for friends, co-workers and loved ones to misunderstand this as laziness, when it's actually caused by fear or from feeling overwhelmed.

> **"It can be difficult for individuals with ADHD to organise themselves"**

It might be scary reading how many difficulties people with ADHD can face, but it's important to remember that with the right support, it doesn't have to hold them back in life.

Strengths associated with ADHD

While ADHD is often characterised by the difficulties it can cause, people with the condition also have a variety of strengths that shouldn't be ignored. For example, people with ADHD are well known for their ability to think outside the box, and for

coming up with creative solutions to a wide variety of problems. They also tend to be extremely resilient and can perform well under pressure, while also having enhanced empathy skills and understanding.

Although there are many difficulties that someone with ADHD might face at work, people with ADHD also possess a number of characteristics that make them excellent employees. This includes being well suited to fast-paced jobs that require effective multitasking and quick thinking. Hyperfocus is also possible when someone with ADHD is assigned to a project or job role that aligns with their interests – this involves a period of intense concentration, which can be very productive and result in completing tasks within a short space of time when there is an imminent deadline. As with all employees, people with ADHD perform best when they are encouraged and supported appropriately and are treated as individuals with unique personalities.

How you can support someone living with ADHD

If someone in your life has ADHD it can be hard to know how to be there for them in a way that is beneficial. It's normal to feel frustrated by some of the symptoms that they face, but you should always remember that this is unintentional, and communicating with patience and kindness will make a huge difference. This is particularly relevant for children and young people, who may not fully understand why they act the way they do. One useful way that friends and family members can support loved ones is by engaging in open and honest conversations about their difficulties, and coming up with collaborative solutions to their problems. Sometimes simply having another person available to complete tasks alongside them can make all the difference. Known as body doubling, this is an effective technique that can help people with ADHD become motivated to tackle tasks that they struggle with.

It can also be helpful to seek professional help. Adults with ADHD can sometimes benefit from cognitive behavioural therapy (CBT), which is a type of talking therapy that focuses on your thoughts and behaviours. In the UK, people with ADHD can also receive support from Access to Work – a government scheme that's set up to help people with a disability or health problem to stay in or gain employment. Other people might prefer ADHD-focused coaching instead of therapy, which can help with the development of practical skills such as problem solving, time management and goal setting. Additional options include parent training and support groups for parents or carers who are supporting a young person. Finally, medication can also have a huge impact on how people with ADHD think and feel. If you or someone you know is struggling, they should speak to their general practitioner or psychiatrist to discuss any potential options.

Whichever the method, accessing appropriate support can be life changing for someone who is neurodivergent, and encourage them to feel more comfortable and confident in their skills and abilities.

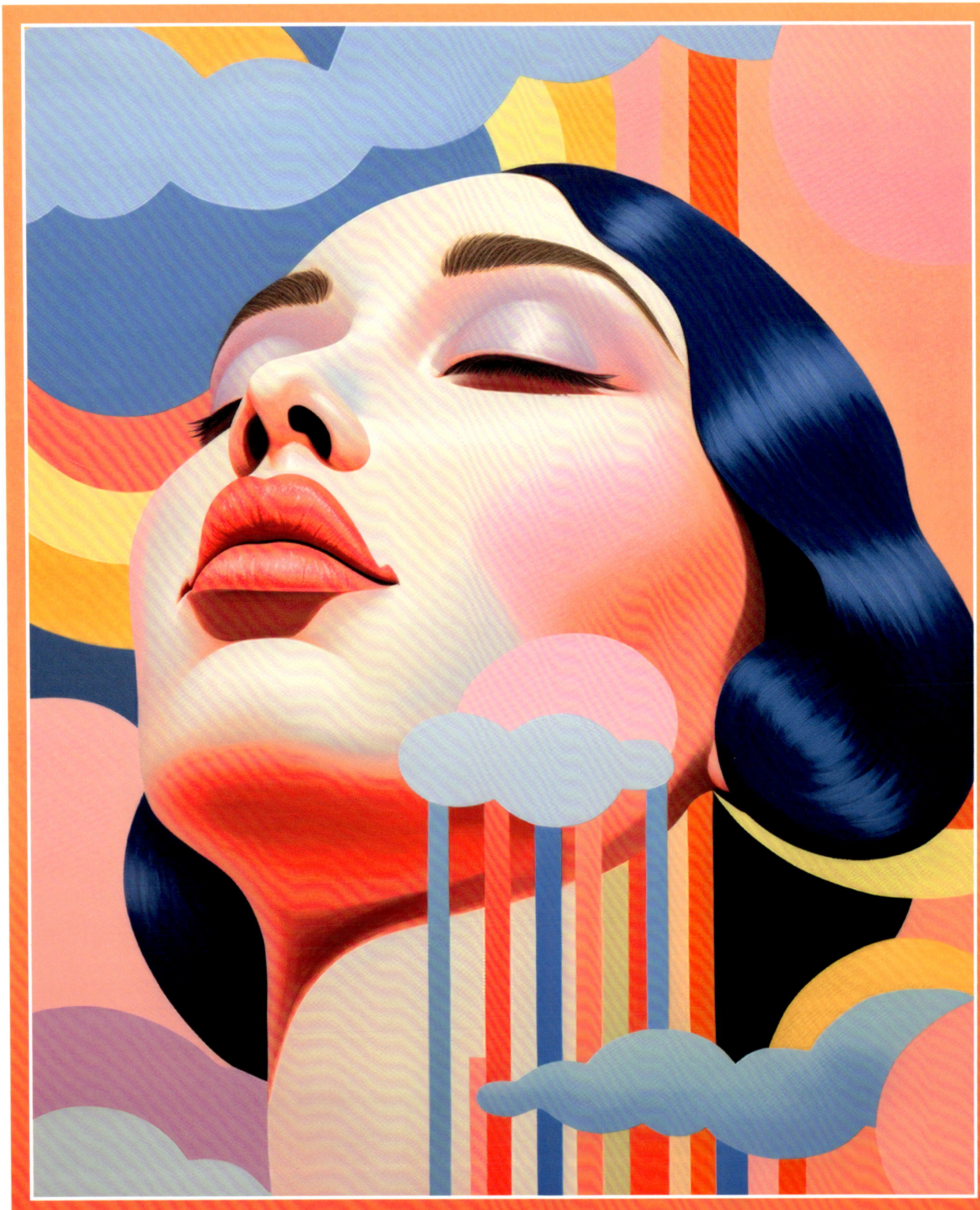

Women, hormones and ADHD

We explore how the menstrual cycle and menopause can impact women who live with ADHD

Words Julie Bassett

We already know that ADHD can present itself differently in women and girls, but did you know that female hormones can also impact ADHD symptoms? Many women find that their ADHD symptoms seem worse at different times of the month, and at different points in their life, which can be linked to the ebb and flow of hormones during a menstrual cycle, as well as the larger changes that happen to hormones during perimenopause, menopause and beyond.

The links between ADHD symptoms and hormones can sometimes be identified at a young age. When a girl hits puberty and starts her periods, it can lead to a change in previously diagnosed ADHD symptoms, or it may trigger a referral for diagnosis as symptoms become more obvious. We don't yet know enough about why this is, but there are theories. One theory is that the sudden surge of hormones can directly impact on ADHD symptoms.

For a girl who has already been diagnosed with ADHD and is on medication that is helping to manage the symptoms, the onset of puberty can lead to bodily changes that can affect the way that medication is metabolised. This means that a previously effective treatment plan and dosage may no longer be working quite as well, leading to a worsening in symptoms.

Menstruation and ADHD

The menstrual cycle can go on to impact women with ADHD of all ages. To understand why ADHD symptoms might change over the course of a month, it helps to understand what happens to hormones during a typical menstrual cycle.

During each cycle, the body goes through four key stages that influence levels of oestrogen and progesterone, the key female sex hormones. The follicular stage is when the body is preparing for ovulation, with high levels of oestrogen and lower levels of progesterone. Next is ovulation, when an egg is released and oestrogen levels hit their peak. Following this is the luteal phase, when the body prepares for the potential implantation of a fertilised egg, lowering oestrogen levels and starting to release more progesterone. If the egg isn't fertilised at this point, both hormones will start to drop, which is around the time that some people get PMS. This then leads to menstruation, which is when you have your period, shedding the thickened lining of the uterus. At this time your hormone levels will

> **"During perimenopause, oestrogen levels start to decline, causing a huge number of symptoms"**

decrease, signalling the end of one cycle and the beginning of another.

A study published in November 2023 in the journal *Hormones and Behaviour* (Ashley G Eng et al), explored a theory and evidence around the link between fluctuating hormones in women through their cycle and a change in ADHD symptoms. It found that ADHD symptoms were more enhanced when oestrogen levels were in decline, in particular mid-cycle when oestrogen builds up and then drops after ovulation, and at the end of a cycle when oestrogen is depleted. The study theorised that mid-cycle, in the lead up to ovulation, those with ADHD were more likely to take bigger risks or seek rewards/dopamine, whereas the end of a cycle was characterised by a reduction in executive function and avoidance behaviours. The theory also suggests that ADHD symptoms are at their lowest during the follicular stage, when hormones are more balanced.

We know that oestrogen contributes to the normal functions of our body and brain. Oestrogen plays an important role in the production of dopamine and serotonin, and when levels are low, this could make existing dysregulation of these neurotransmitters worse.

You might find it useful to keep a symptom diary alongside cycle tracking, as this can help you to identify whether there are patterns between your menstrual cycle and ADHD symptoms.

Perimenopause and menopause

Just as women get into the rhythm of their cycles, along comes perimenopause and menopause, which throws up a new set of challenges. During perimenopause, oestrogen levels start to decline, causing a huge number of symptoms, from hot flushes and irregular periods, to mood changes, anxiety, headaches, insomnia and cognitive issues. Given the link between lower oestrogen levels and worsening ADHD symptoms, it's no wonder that entering the perimenopause stage of life can result in a longer-term progression of the condition.

For women who have a diagnosis already, and have a good understanding of their symptoms, they may be very aware of these changes happening. This can help you to draw on your existing tools or consult with your doctor with regards to increasing medication, for example. For some women, who have been undiagnosed and whose symptoms have been missed or attributed to another cause, perimenopause can actually be the trigger that makes symptoms become more apparent and can even be the reason that a woman seeks a diagnosis. It's not a surprise, then, that for women who were not diagnosed as children, the average age of diagnosis is 36-38 years old - which may be when the body is starting to shift a little more towards perimenopause. Most women start perimenopause in their early- to mid-40s. This stage then continues until menopause, considered a year after the last period, around an average age of 51.

There is some overlap in the symptoms associated with perimenopause and ADHD, such as issues with focus, concentration, memory, mood, anxiety and low self-esteem. This can make it hard to determine what is the root cause of certain behaviours, which can be very frustrating and hard to manage. There are treatments for menopause, such as HRT if suitable, that can help to rebalance hormones, which may help to ease both the symptoms of menopause and the increase in ADHD symptoms.

Beyond perimenopause and menopause - the postmenopause stage - things should settle down again as the body adjusts to its new, lower hormone levels. Some women also find that life gets a little more manageable without the monthly fluctuations in symptoms once the menstrual cycle has ceased.

However, it's important to discuss concerns with a professional or your usual support network, as you may need to change your current treatment plan or support tools to adapt to this new phase of life.

Using hormonal birth control

Another factor for women with ADHD to consider is the impact of any hormonal contraception (HC) they may choose to use, whether this is to prevent unwanted pregnancy or to control other medical conditions, such as irregular or heavy periods, or PCOS. There have been studies that have shown an increased risk of mental health conditions among women who have ADHD and use oral hormonal contraception methods. One study* concluded that: "Girls and young women with ADHD have an increased risk of developing depression when using oral HC compared with their unaffected peers". However, it's important to find a balance - young women with ADHD are more likely to suffer from PMS, for which HC can be a first-line treatment, and the rate of teenage pregnancies is higher among girls and young women with ADHD. There is a lack of research in this area, and family doctors don't routinely give information about the possible side effects of using HC for women with ADHD - in part because there's just not enough information available. It's something to bear in mind and monitor when it comes to deciding on whether to take HC or not.

*Hormonal Contraceptive Use and Risk of Depression Among Young Women With Attention-Deficit/Hyperactivity Disorder. Lundin, C et al. June 2023.

Seeking a diagnosis

Do you think you or your child has ADHD but aren't sure what to do next? Getting a diagnosis is an important first step, but don't feel intimidated – we walk you through the process here

Words Julia Mitchell

While recent years have seen a rise in awareness about the signs and symptoms of ADHD, the process of receiving a diagnosis can sometimes be lengthy, confusing, and even expensive. Navigating the healthcare system doesn't have to be tricky, though, and this article will explain how you can access the support that you or your loved ones need.

Doing the research

There are lots of resources available, and you can find information about a variety of conditions in this title. Other places to look include charities and national health organisations, such as ADHD UK. Other websites can easily be found online, or through books from your local library. Some of the books and websites you look at may have screening tests. These can be useful tools to help you decide whether you or your loved one may have ADHD. Although a diagnosis itself can't be made solely from questionnaires like these, they can be a useful place to start, particularly in the early stages of your journey. It's worth noting here that these tests are not definitive, and regardless of what a questionnaire may say, it's still worth seeking clinical advice if you feel that something isn't right.

Once you have an understanding of the symptoms, it could also be useful to keep a diary of your experiences, noting down what happens, when, and how it makes you feel. Try keeping this diary over the course of a few weeks, and see what you have at the end of it. It might also be helpful to think about the impact that these symptoms have on your life overall, and how gaining a diagnosis might help.

Seeking a diagnosis for a child can often be a slightly different process, and may need to involve their school (if they have one). As their brains are still developing, symptoms can be slightly different in children than with adults, so it's worth taking this into consideration while you are researching. Again, it could be useful to make a note of the symptoms that your child displays, and at what point they started to develop, so that you can take this with you to your medical appointments. This might be something that your child's class teacher or special needs coordinator can help with if they have been displaying symptoms at school. Older children or teenagers may be able to play a more active role in this process by helping with the research and explaining how they feel.

Approaching your GP

When you feel ready, it's time to make an appointment with your general practitioner. This can be a nerve-wracking step, but being prepared will help you to approach the appointment with confidence. It's a good idea to write down a list of symptoms, or reasons why you feel that you might have ADHD, so that you know exactly what you want to talk about in the appointment. This also means that if you get stuck or feel like you're forgetting something, you have something to refer back to. Also, don't be afraid to ask for a second opinion if the appointment doesn't go how you hoped.

The exact process that you follow will be different depending on the healthcare system in your country, but as a general rule, your primary care doctor should refer you to a specialist mental health professional. This could be a psychiatrist, psychologist or paediatrician, for example. It's likely that you and your family members will have to complete a series of questions about your symptoms and how they present. Sometimes you might be asked to complete these at home before your appointment for your doctor to review. This helps the professional to develop a fully rounded view of how you have experienced symptoms throughout your life, which is important for many conditions, such as ADHD, that begin in childhood.

Navigating waiting lists

In the UK, there are often long waiting lists for psychiatric assessments. If you're based in England and the wait using the National Health Service is too long, you may be able to locate an alternative provider for certain conditions using Right to Choose, which should then be paid for by the NHS. You can find out more about this on the Right to Choose website. There are also a variety of private options if you would prefer to go down that route.

It's important to know which mental health professionals are able to diagnose this condition, especially if you are hoping to look privately. In the UK, an adult ADHD diagnosis can only be made by a psychiatrist. Your GP should be able to provide you with the relevant information, which you can also find on the NHS website.

Pros and cons of seeking a diagnosis

Deciding whether or not to pursue a formal diagnosis is a personal choice, and only you can decide whether it's something that's right for you and your family.

There are a wide variety of potential benefits from receiving a diagnosis, including the opportunity to understand yourself or your child better. If the diagnosis is for you, you'll be able to request reasonable adjustments at work, in order to ensure that you have the necessary support to complete your role in a way that works for you. If it's a child or young person who receives the diagnosis, they should be able to access support from their school.

Although receiving a diagnosis can be very beneficial, it can also be highly overwhelming. The process can be long, and might require you to discuss personal information that makes you feel uncomfortable. Others may worry that people will treat them differently once they have a diagnosis, or that they might face discrimination at work. Unfortunately there is still a stigma towards ADHD, and not everyone will understand the implications of your diagnosis. It's also important to consider how you might feel once you've been assessed.

Ultimately, it's up to you whether or not you decide to pursue a diagnosis. Whatever your decision, make sure that you speak to someone you trust, and always remember that you don't have to face it alone.

"It could be useful to make a note of the symptoms that your child displays, and at what point they started to develop"

Are we overdiagnosing ADHD?

Increased awareness has resulted in a rise in diagnoses, but the stats may not be telling the full story

Words Natalia Lubomirski

In addition to a greater awareness of ADHD traits, an increasing number of celebrities are choosing to talk about their midlife ADHD diagnosis in a bid to bust myths about the condition. People are finally gaining a better understanding of their own neurodiversity after many years of being undiagnosed and untreated.

However, with new cases soaring, there's now a big question mark over whether these diagnoses are accurate. Is everyone simply jumping on the ADHD bandwagon?

Defining the condition

For years, ADHD and those living with it have been misunderstood. Until recently there were still misconceptions surrounding how ADHD affects adults - especially women.

Symptoms are categorised in three ways: inattentiveness, hyperactivity/impulsiveness or a combination. This means that the condition can manifest very differently from person to person.

Recent research has also shown that females with ADHD are more likely to be inattentive - rather than have the 'hyperactivity' more commonly seen in males - this can look like daydreaming, scattiness and an inability to regulate emotions, so symptoms can be easily missed. The sad reality is that in the past many women simply slipped through the net.

Rising numbers

The situation has changed somewhat in the last ten years or so, with ADHD diagnoses increasing significantly[1]. "This is mainly due to increased awareness and understanding of the condition," explains Dr Andrea Pickering[2], and individuals wanting answers for how they feel. More people are seeking an assessment due to increased life

Is it anxiety?

"ADHD symptoms are lifelong and tend to fluctuate based on interest levels," explains Dr Vyas-Lee. "Anxiety-related inattention often improves when worries are eased."

demands, which are making symptoms much harder to manage, says clinical psychologist Dr Jenna Vyas-Lee[3]. And now they "finally have the language to describe their symptoms."

The criteria used to diagnose individuals has also broadened to include challenges encountered by adults, as well as highlight the differences between men and women. "This greater focus on inattention rather than hyperactivity and disruptive behaviour has increased recognition of the condition in women," says Dr Pickering.

What's more, people are recognising ADHD traits in themselves after seeing relatable content online, including symptoms shared by celebrities, and then self-referring privately.

False positives

While this has helped some access long-overdue life-changing support, there's now a worry that ADHD may be overdiagnosed, with inadequate assessments to blame.

"Some assessments are relying on quick checklists rather than in-depth evaluations," says Dr Vyas-Lee. "It has led to questions about whether ADHD is being diagnosed too readily, without thorough consideration of other potential explanations."

Symptoms can be hard to interpret. There's no set test to diagnose it, and it can often echo other mental health conditions, such as anxiety, making accurate diagnosis challenging. "ADHD and anxiety can overlap, especially with symptoms like restlessness or difficulty concentrating," says Dr Pickering.

The impact

The recent rise in diagnoses has far-reaching consequences. "For the NHS [the UK's National Health Service], it means longer waiting lists and a surge in demand for ADHD medication," says Dr Vyas-Lee. "For individuals, a diagnosis can be empowering, but only if it's accurate and comes with the right support." Overdiagnosis can risk undermining the incredible gains that have been made for those living with ADHD. It could potentially overwhelm the system, meaning those who really need the help won't be able to access it.

The goal shouldn't be more diagnoses, but the right ones, leading to meaningful support that truly changes lives, says Dr Vyas-Lee. So how can you ensure you receive the right outcome?

Accurate assessment

NICE guidelines state that assessments should be made by healthcare professionals with training and expertise in diagnosing ADHD. Dr Vyas-Lee says a comprehensive assessment should go beyond simple questionnaires and include the following:

- A thorough interview, exploring early childhood behaviours and milestones, and current challenges.

- Information from family members or teachers. Old school reports can be useful.

- Review of mental health conditions, such as autism, anxiety, depression, sleep disorders and trauma – alternative explanations should be considered.

- An assessment of how symptoms impact daily life, and not just whether they are present.

Treatment

Medication is one option, but there are several alternative therapies available:

- Cognitive behavioural therapy (CBT) improves focus, manages emotions and establishes routines.

- Coaching helps with organisation and productivity.

- Lifestyle interventions – sleep, exercise, nutrition and mindfulness.

> "Overdiagnosis can risk undermining the incredible gains that have been made for those living with ADHD"

Symptom tracker

- ☐ Carelessness
- ☐ **Inability to start / finish a task**
- ☐ Boredom
- ☐ **Problems focusing / prioritising**
- ☐ Difficulty remembering instructions / forgetfulness Interrupting others / speaking out of turn
- ☐ **Mood swings**
- ☐ Poor stress management
- ☐ **Risk-taking**

1 According to a study by University College London. 2 clinical-partners.co.uk. 3 koveminds.com.

ADHD in adulthood

As neurodiversity enters the mainstream, more and more adults are seeking, and receiving, diagnoses of neurodiversity. We've spoken to people who have done exactly this...

Words Edoardo Albert

A first cousin of the writer of this article is probably autistic – but he's never been diagnosed and now he never will be. He's become comfortable in his skin and is not looking for any explanations as to why he is the way he is. Besides, as he is 61, for most of his life no such diagnosis would have been possible. He's capable, fluent in language (speaks Italian, German and English) and lives his own life. But he also never realises when he's speaking too loudly, misses social cues and, once fixed on a plan, finds it impossible to change it. These are classic signs for autism today but that wasn't always the case. For most of his life, he wouldn't have been diagnosed with autism even if he had decided to go and see a doctor.

> **"An increasing number of adults are seeking advice about whether they are neurodiverse"**

Autism was only added to the manual of mental disorders, the Diagnostic and Statistical Manual of Mental Disorders (DSM), in 1980. But according to this, he would not have been diagnosed with the condition because the diagnostic criteria included gross distortions or deficits in language and rigid attachment to objects. It was only in 1994, with the fourth edition of the DSM, that he might have been diagnosed with a new subtype of autism, Asperger's syndrome. By then he was 31. So for more than half of his life, no autism diagnosis would have been possible for him.

Now, so far as he is concerned, it's not a matter that interests him. He knows who he is and he doesn't need a label to tell him more.

However, not all adults feel this way. With the increasing acceptance of neurodiversity in wider society, increasing publicity about different conditions, and more and more high-profile people revealing their own neurodivergence, an increasing number of adults are seeking advice about whether they are, after all, neurodiverse. For this article we spoke to Issy Hawkins and Lara Ezekiel to ask why they had sought a diagnosis, what difference the diagnosis had made to their lives, and how it had affected their family and friends.

What made you seek a diagnosis?

Issy Hawkins: I speak a lot online about sobriety and addiction, and addiction is something that has run in my family quite a lot. I'd seen research linking addiction and ADHD, and also eating disorders in women. My family has been troubled with addiction issues and eating disorders so I thought there might be something there, particularly as women are underdiagnosed for ADHD and autism. So in order to understand my family better, and with regard to children that I might have in the future, I wanted to see. It was curiosity more than anything.

Lara Ezekiel: It happened this way: one of my biggest struggles is packing to go on holiday. It's 3am, the taxi has arrived, the house looks like it's been burgled, nothing's fully packed, the children are still asleep and we're on the edge of missing the plane. And I wouldn't have slept for 70 hours beforehand because I've been trying to pack. I always thought it was my fault and I just hadn't tried hard enough.

This time, though, we were going on holiday with my best friend and her family and she saw what I was trying to do. She saw I was on it – but that it just wasn't working.

Then the holiday got worse and worse. There was a point where my friend's husband said I was spoiling everything. I was never able to keep up with them. I was making everyone late. I was really down and I looked up about my issues and I read about executive dysfunction, which then led me

to ADHD. But I thought I definitely didn't have ADHD because that was boys that can't keep still. But when I got home I did an online test and it came up that I had ADHD. And all the questions: they sounded like me. They were all Lara-isms. That's what my friends called it when I did stuff that other people didn't. I just thought that was me.

My whole life I was different. But when I was younger my friends accommodated me. My husband, who I've been with since I was 18, is great, so I've been lucky that way. I had a tumultuous upbringing. I remember when I was in year five lying on the floor crying my eyes out because I couldn't complete the homework because it had taken so long. Then at secondary school, the comments were always about me not being able to finish stuff – although I also never got to school on time. Almost every day I missed the first lesson. Then, from 17, I lived on my own and I thought my struggles were to do with that. I went to schools which were pretty wild so I didn't stand out as much as I might have done at more normal schools. After school, I became a professional dancer. But I had so much frustration and self-hatred because I was never able to get past go.

The admin was the hardest. I was two hours late for my own wedding although, ironically, that wasn't my fault. After I got married, I realised there were ten years of unopened letters – so many fines and things.

The lateness was always the biggest thing because that impacts everyday life. They see it as me being late but what they don't see is what is going on behind the scenes.

How old were you when you went to your doctor about this?

IH: I was 31.

LE: I was 35 and a half when I went to the GP and I was diagnosed at 37.

Was it straightforward getting a diagnosis?

IH: No, it wasn't. I found my doctor was very dismissive. He made me cry on the phone because he made it out to be some sort of fad: "Everybody wants to be diagnosed with ADHD now". This, despite there having been a lot of suffering in my family, so I found that quite upsetting. He was gatekeeping and claimed that there was a huge waiting list and there were no providers anyway in my area. Luckily, I had researched my right to choose, and I suggested a provider who would be able to see me in three months. I had to hound them to refer me. They kept on trying to refer me to a different provider and I kept on having to say no because the waiting list there was too long. It was a really difficult process but I needed to go via the NHS pathway as I wanted to make sure I could get help afterwards.

Because my GP put so many obstacles in my path I very nearly said, "Okay, just don't worry about it".

LE: It was easier in my case, although I had to wait a year and a half for the referral. I went to the GP and he said, "Okay, I'll pass you on".

Find a way forward

NHS assessment is all very well but what do you do if your GP refuses to refer you? Unfortunately, a significant number of people have encountered this problem. However, it's not the end of the road; there are other ways to get your diagnosis.

If your GP refuses to make a referral, you are within your rights to ask for a second opinion. You can make a formal request for a second opinion or you could simply make another appointment but ask to see a different GP at the practice. If you do the latter, you do need to tell the doctor about your previous conversation.

Should there be no other GPs available at your practice, you can change practice. You could also decide to have a private assessment for the condition. Unlike an NHS assessment, you will have to pay for this. However, you will usually be seen much more quickly (although do check that they are professionally recognised).

An important option available to NHS patients in England is the right to choose the people providing you with healthcare. Should the waiting time be too long, the distance too far or the tester not sympathetic to your needs, then you can ask for an alternative test provider.

How did you find the testing procedure?

IH: It was an online appointment. At the start I had to prove who I was by showing my driver's licence which, as anyone with ADHD will tell you, is no easy matter for us. After I had finally found it, there were some forms to fill in. They also needed someone who knew me well to fill in a report about me. The whole thing took about an hour.

LE: The questions the tester asked were brilliant. At the end she said, "I don't think it will come as any surprise to you to learn that you have ADHD". The funny thing was, when my dad had to fill in the form for what I was like as a child, he kept on saying, "But that's normal". I'm now positive my dad has ADHD too.

What difference has having this diagnosis made to your lives?

IH: In terms of understanding myself and some of my family, it's made quite a big difference. But I had already had to come up with coping mechanisms long before my diagnosis because I had to deal with addiction issues myself.

There was some grief. If it had been caught earlier – when I was a teenager, when I really struggled emotionally – then it's possible that my life would have been easier.

LE: Completely life changing. By the time I went to the referral I thought I had ADHD but there was still a niggling doubt. When I knew it was true I went away and learned and learned – and learned about my life. It all made sense now. I realised how much self-hate I had from trying and failing so much. But then I knew I wasn't the only one and it wasn't my fault. I really had been trying. It wasn't that I hadn't been trying enough.

Since then, I have gone even deeper into ADHD and ways to live with it; I must have read hundreds, thousands of books and articles about it. I volunteered for my local NHS group to help others who've just had a diagnosis of ADHD. I saw the struggles of the ADHDers and in most cases what it came down to was admin. Their lives were being ruined because of admin. So with all the research I had done, I was able to help them. That's made a huge difference to me – and them too, I hope.

> **"If it had been caught earlier it's possible that my life would have been easier"**

Has your diagnosis made a difference for the people around you, your family and friends?

IH: My husband was pretty certain I had it. He'd already done research on ADHD and understands that sometimes I get overwhelmed and knows in those situations he needs to be a bit more supportive.

What's been most interesting is seeing other people in my family get diagnosed. It has allowed us to understand why things happen the way they do and not get frustrated.

There's also a lot of conversations going back over things that happened. I'm one of four children and there were many emotional meltdowns, obsessive behaviours, eating disorders and addiction issues. Now we're saying, "Do you remember that time when...?" and it all starts to make sense. It's given us a key to understand a lot of the things that happened in the past.

LE: After I got diagnosed, I went around telling people, telling everyone: this is me. This is the reason for all the Lara-isms. I didn't want to be in trouble anymore for things I couldn't help. Some people were interested. Some weren't. If they weren't, I let that go. It definitely helped my husband, him knowing, and my best friend, it helped her too.

And most importantly, I don't want my children to go through what I went through. Neurodiversity runs in families so they'll probably have their own issues. But at least I understand it all better now. And I have big plans for ways to make a future where neurodiverse and neurotypical people stand side by side.

Fashion or freedom?

Rates of diagnosis of all the different types of neurodivergence has surged over the last decade but none has increased as dramatically as ADHD. In 2012, the NHS prescribed medication for ADHD for 8,000 people, of whom more than 6,000 were children. By 2022 that number had surged to 26,000, with the gap between adults and children narrowing rapidly. This is just the number of people prescribed drugs to treat ADHD; the number with a diagnosis but who have opted not to use medication is much larger.

This rise has prompted concerns that it's all just a social-media trend. On TikTok, there are millions of posts tagged #adhd and they've had billions of views. Some doctors have worried people are diagnosing themselves through online questionnaires, while others suggest that there are now social benefits to labelling yourself with a neurodiversity, particularly one like ADHD, that has plenty of celebrities sporting their ADHD badges.

However, since the National Institute for Health and Care Excellence estimates that five per cent of the children in the UK have ADHD, and between three and four per cent of the adult population have it, then even with the current steep rise in diagnoses, it remains true that the great majority of people with ADHD have not been formally diagnosed.

This holds even truer for people with less 'fashionable' neurodivergences. Estimates suggest that around 15% of the UK population, which is one person in seven, has some form of neurodiversity. This would mean that the majority of neurodivergent people in Britain, and also around the world, have no formal diagnosis of their condition. Some will know that they stand out from the crowd and, where knowledge of the different forms of neurodiversity has spread widely, they might well be able to label it. But in many cases, these people will carry on in silence, struggling alone, ascribing all their difficulties to some failure in themselves rather than knowing that it's a feature of the way they are made.

If there is one reason to be grateful for the spread of #adhd and #autism and other similar tags on social media, it's for the fact that more and more people are seeing their difficulties reflected in the lives of other people and realising that, no, they're not alone and that it's not their fault.

Treatments and coping mechanisms

Covering medication, talking therapies and self-help strategies, here are some of the ways that you can manage the symptoms of ADHD

Words Julia Mitchell

While life with ADHD can sometimes feel challenging, accessing the right support can help people with the condition to live happy and fulfilling lives. This will look different for everyone, and can involve a combination of tools such as medication, talking therapies, coaching, and self-help strategies.

As it's common for this to be a trial-and-error process, it's important to approach finding the most effective treatment with patience and self-compassion. Although it can be difficult, there will always be someone you can speak to - whether that's a friend, family member or medical professional.

Medication

A controversial topic for some, the decision of whether to take medication for ADHD is personal and varies between individuals. You may recognise brand names such as Adderall (amphetamine/dextroamphetamine) and Ritalin (methylphenidate), both of which are commonly prescribed stimulant medications prescribed to people with ADHD. Other non-stimulant options are also available for people who would prefer not to take, or do not respond to stimulant medication. Examples of non-stimulant medications include atomoxetine, guanfacine, viloxazine, and clonidine.

It's important to discuss the options thoroughly with a psychiatrist, and to weigh up any potential benefits with any possible risks. As with all medications, it's common for people to experience side effects - particularly in the first few weeks of taking a new medication or adjusting to a new dose. Side effects can include a decrease in appetite, stomach pain, sleep disturbances and headaches when taking stimulant medication, while non-stimulants can cause fatigue, stomach pain, decreased appetite and nausea. Everyone responds to medication differently, though, so don't be disheartened if it takes a few tries to identify the most effective option.

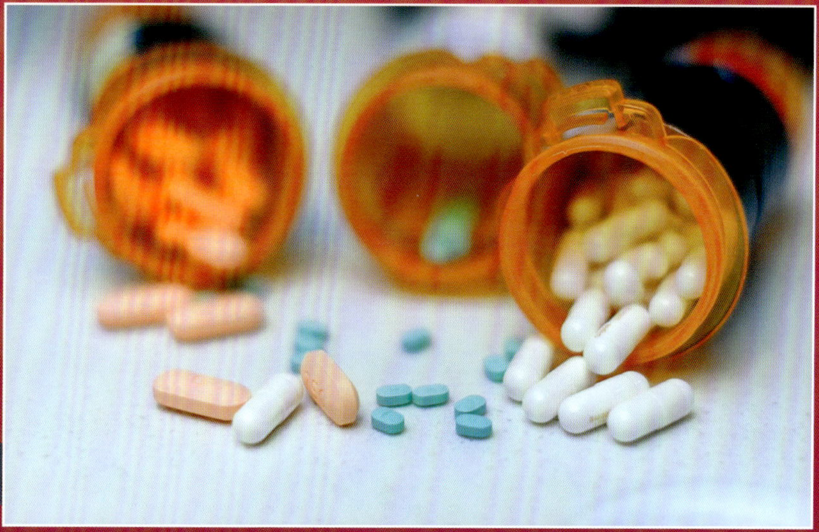

Talking therapies and coaching

As with many other psychological conditions, people with ADHD can often benefit from talking therapies like cognitive behavioural therapy (CBT). This modern form of therapy is evidence-based and focuses on how thoughts and behaviours might maintain someone's difficulties, such as low mood or low self-esteem, with the goal of implementing changes that can help them to feel better. This differs considerably from other forms of therapy like counselling, which is less skills-based, and instead provides an open space for individuals to speak about life experiences and emotional difficulties. This approach can also be useful for people with ADHD, and give people the opportunity to discuss their diagnosis, if that's something that feels important to them.

As an alternative to traditional therapy, coaching is another service that may be beneficial for people with ADHD. Coaching itself typically focuses more on developing practical skills and less on the emotional impact of someone's difficulties. For example, ADHD coaching may include working on organisation skills, time management, problem solving, and goal setting. Although there is currently less research about the effectiveness of coaching as an intervention, recent studies have found favourable results, suggesting that many people have been able to develop practical skills as a result of regular coaching sessions. There are many ways that coaching can be useful for someone with ADHD, although formal therapy might be more appropriate if they are experiencing signs of mental illness such as generalised anxiety disorder or depression.

When seeking a psychological therapist, it's important to make sure that you find someone who is accredited. You can do this by accessing the British Association for Behaviour and Cognitive Psychotherapies (BABCP) and the British Association for Counselling and Psychotherapy (BACP) websites for their list of licensed clinicians. Coaching, on the other hand, is less formally regulated, which can make it challenging to find someone who is adequately experienced and qualified. As a starting point, it may be worth accessing an ADHD charity's website as they can often provide suggestions or advice for finding a suitable coach.

> “Changes to everyday life can make a big difference, such as putting a daily to-do list on the front door”

Self-help strategies for ADHD

While formal support such as medication and talking therapies can be useful for managing life with ADHD, it's also important to explore the variety of self-coping strategies that are available. This can include making the most of technology and the many tools that have been developed to help individuals to stay organised in a busy world. This can be as simple as utilising a calendar app on your mobile phone or tablet, and setting notifications to remind you of important events and activities. Google Keep also comes highly recommended for individuals with ADHD, and can be used to jot down thoughts and ideas as they arise. Not only does this help individuals to remember their thoughts, but it can also help to mitigate impulsivity by providing a place for people to write their thoughts down rather than saying them out loud.

Other ways of utilising technology can include taking photos of things that need to be remembered, instead of relying on pieces of paper that are likely to get lost. Similarly, it can also be useful for people to take photos of things that they want to buy, which they can look at and decide on later instead of purchasing impulsively. Meditation apps like Headspace or Calm can also be incredibly helpful. These applications provide guided meditations that can help people with ADHD to calm their minds, slow down their thoughts, and inject mindful moments into their day.

While modern technology can be an invaluable tool for someone with ADHD, other coping strategies exist that don't require the use of an electronic device. Sometimes simple changes to everyday life can make a big difference, such as putting a daily to-do list on the front door so that it's seen regularly

Making the most of fidget toys

Although most of the current research is focused on children, and the outcomes of those studies show mixed results, fidget toys can be a useful tool for adults who struggle with inattentiveness. Fidgeting itself has been scientifically shown to improve cognitive function, with studies finding that people with ADHD can focus more effectively when keeping their hands occupied.

The toys themselves come in a wide variety of shapes and sizes, including more discreet options, which adults may find preferable. Examples include toys that are small enough to fit into a pocket or desk drawer, and others that are connected to rings or key chains.

Each type of fidget toy offers a unique sensory experience, so it might be worth trying a few to find which is the most effective. These can then be used in a variety of settings to aid concentration, including in meetings, lectures and other situations that require extended periods of focus.

When selecting a fidget toy, it's important to find something that helps the body to fidget, but isn't too distracting, and won't take your attention away from the task at hand. Because of this you may wish to stay away from fidget toys that are brightly coloured or noisy to play with.

"Research shows that regular exercise can be beneficial to people with ADHD"

during the day. It can also be useful to allocate places in the home where items are kept consistently, for example, by keeping important documents together and placing keys in a pot on the hallway table. Items like fidget toys can also be handy for people who struggle with inattentiveness and struggle to sit still. While some fidgets are designed more with children in mind, a variety of tools exist that vary in texture and subtlety.

As with a variety of other conditions, research shows that regular exercise can be beneficial to people with ADHD. It's widely agreed that engaging in aerobic exercise stimulates dopamine and norepinephrine - both neurotransmitters that are involved in regulating the attention system. As an additional incentive, exercise can also help with comorbidities such as anxiety and depression, which commonly accompany ADHD. With a wide variety of options available, people with ADHD are encouraged to engage in a sport or activity of their choice, whether that's cycling, skateboarding, aqua aerobics, or something else.

How parents and guardians can help children with ADHD

Creating structure that leaves room for flexibility can be incredibly helpful for both adults and children. For example, parents can ensure that key parts of their child's day, such as bedtime and mealtimes, are consistent, while allowing additional time for breaks. Parents or guardians can also help children with ADHD to break down their tasks into smaller, more manageable pieces. This is a skill that can follow individuals into their teenage years and beyond, and is particularly useful for completing lengthy tasks like essays or reports.

Making tasks more interesting can also be helpful for children who struggle with inattentiveness. For example, you can try turning household chores into games - set up a timer and see how much they can tidy up in ten minutes. Decreasing distractions can also help with focus, and many children will be entitled to additional time or support during exams at school. Above all, believing in your child, listening to their difficulties and minimising the use of negative language can be transformative in helping a young person to thrive with ADHD.

Adaptations for the classroom

As with many areas of life, children and young people with ADHD often benefit from adaptations to the classroom environment. For young children, this can include establishing strong routines, and providing additional supervision for those who may need extra help to stay on track. One simple way of improving the physical classroom environment can include reducing potential distractions. Other useful suggestions include allowing time in the day for physical movement, for example fetching a drink of water or running an errand, as well as time for play and help with transitions.

As the children become older, it can be useful for students with ADHD to access time extensions for exams and coursework, or even staggered deadlines that require them to submit work gradually over a period of time. Support with taking notes may also be helpful, and this can be achieved by providing the student with recording equipment that can be used in class, or even with a notetaker.

It's worth remembering that all individuals with ADHD will present differently, and have their own unique combination of strengths and difficulties. Because of this, classroom adaptations can look different for everyone and need to be tailored to the individual.

Does CBD (cannabidiol) help with ADHD?

CBD products have become enormously popular in recent years for a wide range of conditions and are sold around the world in a variety of forms. Originating from the cannabis plant, CBD differs as it doesn't contain THC, which is what causes the substance to be psychoactive. This means that CBD oil typically does not make users feel 'high' and is not used in the same way as cannabis, which is illegal in many parts of the world including much of the US and the UK. When purchasing CBD products, it's important to make sure that the substance is legal and purchased from a reputable seller.

When it comes to ADHD, the current scientific research does not recommend using CBD to help with ADHD symptoms. A relatively new area of study, there is currently not enough evidence to show how CBD use impacts people with ADHD and whether it is safe. Although there may be some compelling personal stories out there, previous research into the use of cannabis has even shown that it can have a negative effect, with one study finding that cannabis use may impact on the executive functioning of young people under the age of 16, which includes those with ADHD. Ultimately, whether or not to try CBD as a way of managing ADHD is a personal choice, but is currently not recommended, and there are many alternative strategies and medications that have been thoroughly tested.

Overall, the key to managing ADHD is often to implement a number of coping techniques and strategies, while making sure to access additional support when necessary.

Comorbidities

How other conditions present with ADHD, including a range of comorbidities such as autism, dyslexia, anxiety and depression

Words Julia Mitchell

Neurodiversities

ADHD often occurs alongside other neurodiversities such as Autistic Spectrum Disorder, with research finding that around 21% of children with ADHD also have autism and many more have autistic traits.

Known as AuDHD, people with both conditions may experience conflict between the two, particularly as ADHD often causes impulsivity and a need for novelty, whereas autism usually craves routine and similarity. But similarities do exist between ADHD and autism, including a heightened focus on special interests, trouble getting things done day-to-day and rejection sensitivity. Treatment to help manage the conditions can include talking therapies and medication.

Many people with ADHD also experience Tourette syndrome or other tic disorders. A widely misunderstood condition that doesn't necessarily include swearing or profanities, Tourette's usually starts in childhood and involves a combination of motor and vocal tics. While treatment is not always needed, there are specific types of psychological therapy used to treat tics, including habit reversal training and exposure with response prevention.

Anxiety and depression

As two of the most common mental health conditions, anxiety and depression frequently occur alongside ADHD. To put that in perspective, it's thought that around one in three people with ADHD also have depression, while up to one in two people with ADHD also have an anxiety disorder.

Anxiety and depression can sometimes develop as a result of ADHD symptoms, such as low self-esteem or feelings of being overwhelmed, although it can also develop independently. As many of the symptoms can overlap between the three conditions, some people may find that they are initially misdiagnosed prior to receiving an ADHD diagnosis. Examples of overlapping symptoms include difficulties concentrating and fidgeting, which can be symptoms of anxiety, while struggles with organisation and accomplishing tasks day-to-day are common signs of depression.

The good news is that there are many effective treatments available for helping with anxiety and depression, ranging from specialist medications, to talking therapies such as cognitive behavioural therapy and counselling.

Learning difficulties

Learning difficulties are thought to impact between 30-50% of people with ADHD and refer to a specific difficulty in an area of learning. Examples of commonly experienced learning difficulties include dyslexia, dyspraxia, dysgraphia and dyscalculia - four similar-sounding conditions that present differently and can also occur together.

Although the symptoms of each can be complex, dyslexia usually presents with difficulties in reading and writing, while the lesser-known dysgraphia is specifically related to challenges in producing written work. Dyscalculia on the other hand is frequently identified by difficulties with numeracy skills, and dyspraxia most often impacts motor skills and spacial awareness. Similarly to ADHD, these difficulties first present in childhood and tend to last throughout someone's life.

Once again, the symptoms of ADHD and learning difficulties often overlap, and it can take a while to reach the most accurate diagnoses. It's important to remember that learning difficulties do not describe general intelligence, and that support is widely available, particularly in schools where young people may require individualised support and resources.

Oppositional defiant disorder (ODD)

A condition most frequently experienced in childhood, around 40% of children with ADHD will develop ODD, although many outgrow this by adulthood.

Some of the most identifiable symptoms of ODD include frequent arguing, high levels of aggression, and a tendency to ignore instructions - all of which occur regularly over a span of six months. Although it's not known exactly why the two disorders co-occur, experts have suggested that poor impulse control associated with ADHD can lead to children also developing ODD.

There may also be a genetic link, and environmental risk factors, such as difficulties at home and inconsistencies in discipline, can also contribute to the development of ODD.

Although the symptoms of ODD can be difficult to manage, effective treatments are available. These will usually involve a combination of cognitive behavioural therapy, counselling and medication, while also ensuring that the ADHD

symptoms themselves are well managed. It is important to note that many symptoms of ODD are ones that are commonly experienced as children grow, and therefore do not always indicate a diagnosable mental health condition.

Conduct disorder (CD)

In some cases, children and young people with ADHD will also develop CD, which can be similar to ODD but tends to be more severe. Common symptoms include physical aggression towards people or animals, bullying and destructive behaviour such as arson or vandalism, lying or stealing from others and knowingly breaking rules or laws. Crucially, CD can also lead to further conditions, such as antisocial personality disorder, mood disorders or substance abuse, if it is left to go untreated.

Potential support for CD can include medication and cognitive behavioural therapy, which can help individuals to change the ways that they think and behave. Family-based therapy may also be beneficial for people who are experiencing CD.

As with other conditions, it's thought that genetic and environmental factors can cause the disorder to develop, particularly as it often runs in families, or occurs within family units where other disorders or substance abuse are present. Difficulties at home, including instability and trauma, are also risk factors for young people developing CD.

Sensory processing disorder (SPD)

Sensory processing disorder refers to instances where people react differently to sensory input. This can include feeling much more sensitive to stimuli, such as light, sound and touch, while others may describe the opposite and experience a reduced sensitivity. The former is known as hypersensitivity, while the latter is called hyposensitivity.

"The symptoms of ADHD and learning difficulties often overlap"

Specific examples of how hypersensitivity can manifest include having a lower pain threshold, showing a dislike to hugs or soft touches and difficulties with foods of certain textures. Hyposensitivity, on the other hand, may result in a reduced sensitivity to pain, difficulties in understanding personal space, frequently touching things or putting them to their mouth, as well as bumping into things and people.

It's thought that SPD can develop as a result of early life complications, like a premature birth, low birth weight and alcohol or drug consumption during pregnancy. It can also develop due to ADHD and autism, with studies finding that up to 40% of children with ADHD or SPD have both conditions.

Sleep disorders

ADHD can make it difficult to receive a fulfilling night's sleep, as it's known to make it more challenging to fall asleep, stay asleep and wake up in the morning. Some people with ADHD may describe themselves as a 'night owl', or report having difficulties shutting their brain off in the evening or feeling restless.

Treatment for sleep difficulties with ADHD most often include implementing good sleep hygiene, such as avoiding naps during the day, having a set bedtime, only using the bedroom for sleep or sex and avoiding caffeine late at night. It may also be useful to keep a sleep diary, which records how many hours the individual is asleep each night, identifying their habits and whether there are any behavioural changes that can be made. Medication such as melatonin and antidepressants can also be helpful in some cases.

Other examples of sleep disorders that commonly occur in people with ADHD include insomnia; circadian rhythm sleep disorders; sleep-disordered breathing; restless leg syndrome and narcolepsy.

Your mental health masterclass

With neurodiversity comes the feeling of being different – and that can lead to struggles with our mental wellbeing

Words Natalia Lubomirski

Despite a staggering one in four people in the UK experiencing a mental health problem each year, the invisible nature of it means there's often a tendency to ignore problems and just get on with it. But, as Stephen Buckley, head of information at mental health charity Mind, says, "Mental health is just like our physical health: everybody has it and we need to take care of it."

He adds, "Thankfully, we've seen the national conversation on mental health move forward, but those with mental health problems still face barriers." The topic remains taboo, especially for older generations - a YouGov survey revealed 25% of over-55s think it's more difficult for them to discuss mental health than younger people. Some 71% felt this was because, in the past, anxiety and depression were seen as weaknesses, rather than health conditions.

Road to recovery

These figures are no surprise, especially knowing what we do about neurodiversity and co-morbidities. But it's how we deal with it that's important. Thankfully, there are things we can do. "Eating healthily, sleeping well, exercising and seeking help are all key," says Stephen. "Different treatments work for different people and the journey to recovery won't always be easy."

Over the following pages, Mind shares advice on how to cope with feelings of anxiety, depression and OCD.

Depression

What is it? In its mildest form, it means being repeatedly in low spirits - at its most severe, it can be life-threatening, making you feel suicidal.

The impact? Symptoms can include "feeling low, numb, worthless or without hope," says Stephen. "You may sleep too much or too little, and withdraw from social contact."

Help yourself List activities, people and places that make you feel good, and try to find ways to bring these things into your daily routine.

Do something new This can boost your mood and break

> **"The invisible nature of it means there's a tendency to ignore problems"**

unhelpful, negative patterns of thinking. You could also try volunteering - it makes you feel better and less alone.

Try self-help Explore cognitive behavioural therapy.

Anxiety

What is it? Feeling anxious is a natural response when we feel under threat. But if you regularly experience anxiety, including panic attacks, which are strong, last a long time and are difficult to control, you may need help.

The impact? You avoid situations that may make you feel anxious. You'll find it hard to go about your everyday life or do things you enjoy.

Help yourself Focus on breathing, especially during a panic attack. Inhale through your nose and out through your mouth, counting from one to five.

> **"It's thought that around three million people in the UK have an anxiety disorder"**

Try complementary and alternative therapies, including meditation, aromatherapy, massage, yoga and reflexology, to aid relaxation.

Not sure if you have a problem? Read on to find out more about the secret signs of anxiety.

Obsessive compulsive disorder (OCD)

What is it? An anxiety disorder with obsessions (unwelcome thoughts, urges and worries that appear in your mind, making you feel anxious) and compulsions (repetitive activities to reduce anxiety, such as checking a door is locked or repeating phrases).

The impact? You might avoid situations that trigger it, including work or seeing friends or family. You may feel ashamed of your thoughts or feel the need to hide your OCD.

Help yourself Talk to someone you trust or write down feelings to discuss together.

Learn to relax Manage stress and try techniques such as deep breathing or mindfulness.

Try peer support This brings together people who have had similar experiences. It helps you feel accepted and confident.

No more feeling anxious!

Millions of us are experiencing anxiety, often without even realising it. Most of us probably think we know what anxiety feels like. Your heart races, you're short of breath, and your body is bathed in a sheen of sweat. But there are plenty of hidden signs, too. Follow this advice on how to spot the hidden signs and do something about it.

"Anxiety is what we feel when we are worried, tense or afraid," says Nicky Lidbetter, CEO of Anxiety UK. It can be caused by a number of factors, including feelings of uncertainty, physical health problems, stress, and your childhood experiences. It's thought that around three million people in the UK have an anxiety disorder, and while clammy hands and a pounding heart could signal anxiety, some signs are less obvious. Here are the more subtle symptoms to look out for...

You over-dramatise small failures

"There's a catastrophising nature to anxiety that makes you perceive things being much worse than they actually are," says Nicky. If you're overdramatic, you may have an over-the-top reaction to a small failing, which could lead to a meltdown or cause you to stay at home for the next few days, unable to face the world.

You're critical of yourself and others

"Being anxious leads to you being hard on yourself. It thrives on the lack of self-esteem you have for yourself and, as a result, you become self-critical and critical of those around you," says Nicky.

You can't sleep

When we're in an anxious state, it can be hard for our body and mind to relax, and we can have trouble sleeping, which can lead to bouts of insomnia.

You're distracted

"We may be preoccupied with our thoughts and easily distracted," explains Nicky. Experiencing racing thoughts is extremely common with anxiety, but this attention to the 'inner dialogue' can result in others perceiving us as distant.

You overthink

"When you're anxious, you're desperately trying to make sense of a situation. Overthinking and labouring over every eventuality is a way of protecting yourself and gaining control," says Nicky.

You're afraid to take risks

Sticking to your 'comfort zone' means you won't have to face frustration, embarrassment, sadness, anger or disappointment – all extreme feelings for someone with anxiety. "When we're anxious, we want to protect ourselves and can see risks as threats, so we become risk-averse," says Nicky.

You talk too much

You may be in a 'high-functioning' state when you're anxious, meaning your mind is going at 100mph. As a result, your actions – such as talking a lot – may follow suit.

> **"Trying to hide symptoms from others can impact physical health"**

You're unwilling to make friends

Opening yourself up emotionally can make you feel vulnerable and exposed. You may already be imagining losing that friendship before it's even started. "Anxiety may isolate us by way of protecting ourselves from unknown territory," says Nicky.

You feel unwell

Constant anxiety has a big effect on the immune system, and trying to hide symptoms from others can impact physical health. "Anxiety can make us fatigued and even sick. Plus, adrenaline released can have a negative impact on our stomachs, as well as other parts of the body," explains Nicky.

When it's more serious...

Seek additional help and support if anxiety is disrupting your day-to-day life and stopping you from doing activities you previously enjoyed.

Shortcuts to serenity

These quick tips can help, so make sure you practise them daily:

- A person who feels they are not worth listening to will speak quickly, because they don't want to keep others waiting on something not worth listening to. A person in authority speaks slowly; even if you don't feel very confident, try slowing down and see how it feels.

- Too much to do? Write down each task you can't do right now on a separate piece of paper. Then, every other day, take a random one and do it. You'll soon get through the list.

- Learn to recognise negative self-talk ('I can't run any more, I've got to stop'). Visualise it as an irritating bug, stamp on it, kill it, then replace it with a positive one ('Come on, I can do this! Only half a mile left!').

- Laugh often. Watch a funny film or a YouTube video and have a good belly laugh. Science shows it helps to lower the stress hormone cortisol and can shift a low mood.

- You are what you do, so if you change what you do, you change what you are. Act in a positive way, take action instead of telling yourself you can't. Talk to people in a positive way. You'll soon start to notice a difference.

- If you choose to say 'no' to something, mentally rehearse the conversation beforehand, saying it simply and directly, giving no more than one key reason. Do not get into explaining or arguing: just repeat 'No, because...' quietly and firmly.

- Before always saying 'yes' to demands, take a deep breath, so you can touch base with yourself to discover what you would truly, honestly prefer to do.

- Have a list of useful apps that benefit your mental health. Try Headspace, Stress & Anxiety Companion, and Catch It.

- Don't aim too high. Set a goal you know you can achieve, then achieve it. You'll feel good. Now set another and achieve that. Soon you'll be setting bigger goals and achieving those, too.

- Visualise yourself at your most confident, then link this feeling to a physical action, such as pinching your thumb and forefinger together. Next time you need to feel confident in a situation, pinch your thumb and finger together to get back to that positive mental state.

- Keep talking. Having a chat with a loved one, sending a text to a friend, or going for a walk with a colleague can boost a low mood.

- Standing tall and straight makes you feel better about yourself. Imagine a piece of string is pulling the top of your head towards the sky, and the rest of your body straightens accordingly.

- Immerse yourself in nature. So-called 'green therapy', being outdoors is a powerful mood-lifter. A Stanford University study showed that a 90-minute walk in nature reduced ruminations, which is a risk factor for mental illness.

How to be calm

"If you're feeling anxious, there are ways you can step back and take control before the symptoms build up and take over," says Nicky.

Use a grounding technique

There are many different exercises and soothing techniques that you can use to distract yourself when you're feeling anxious. Over the page, we've shared some of our tried-and-tested breathing and grounding techniques.

Try positive affirmations

Tell yourself, 'I am safe, I am in control, this feeling is anxiety', and repeat until you feel more in control of your feelings.

Make dietary changes

Small changes to your diet can make a difference to anxiety symptoms. Try eating less processed food, drinking less alcohol, and cutting back or stopping caffeine. Don't forget that caffeine can be present in chocolate and soft drinks, too.

Get enough sleep

Maintain a regular sleeping pattern by going to bed at the same time each night, switching off screens at least one hour before bedtime, and ensuring your bedroom is dark and the right temperature.

Grounding techniques to manage anxiety

Things to do to stop your mind spinning out of control

Words Edoardo Albert

Many studies over the years have proven what most of us predicted all along: anxiety rates are much higher among the neurodiverse than the neurotypical. Chronic anxiety is bad enough, but sometimes these thoughts and feelings can spiral out of control, leading to a full-on panic attack.

Panic attacks are deeply scary. While gripped by one, it can feel as if you are about to die. So it is important to find techniques and exercises that can calm us down from a panic attack.

There are many different techniques but they all work towards bringing us out of a panicked mental state and into the immediate present - where there is no danger. Different techniques work for different people so it might be necessary to try a few before you find something that works best for you. It is best to practise them before a panic attack so that you know the exercise: after all, the middle of a panic attack is not the best time to be trying to remember what to do next.

5-4-3-2-1 technique

During a panic attack, or when we can feel anxiety ramping up, the body and brain are locked into a feedback loop. Feelings of anxiety make the deep brain think it is in danger, which leads to it pumping out emergency hormones while getting the body ready to fight or flee. These elevated physical levels feed the physical sensations that accompany anxiety, making us more anxious, which leads to the deep brain pumping out even more emergency hormones. But all of this is going on inside us. In reality, there is no danger. Even if the anxiety trigger is something like a forthcoming event, the event is not happening yet: there is no need to panic right now. However, the deep part of the brain does not know this.

Future fear has translated into a panic attack in the present. If we can pull our focus back to the present, where in fact there is nothing dangerous, then the body can respond in turn. The 5-4-3-2-1 technique is a way of dissolving future fears into the immediate reality of our surroundings. To begin, as an immediate calming technique, slow the breath. Breathe in for a count of four and then out for a count of four. Repeat this.

Keep this breathing pattern throughout the exercise but the next time you breathe out, look around your surroundings and say, out loud, the names of five things you can see. They could be in the room with you - the chair, a bookcase - or outside, visible through a window - a tree, the sky, someone passing by.

Then, again speaking out loud, say the names of four things you can hear. They can be things loud or quiet, near or far. The point is to focus the attention in your ears at this point.

The third step is to say three things you can feel. This could be the chair under your bottom to the weight of clothes on your shoulder to the touch of a breeze on the cheek. We are working our way through the five senses, employing each sense in turn to divert our attention from the thoughts and feelings inside our mind to the exterior world immediately around us - a world which is calm and safe. By going through the senses in turn, we are conveying a message to our amygdala, which listens to the senses much more closely than it listens to our conscious thoughts, that everything is all right.

The fourth step is to name two things we can smell. For those who don't have particularly sensitive senses of smell it might work to carry around something that has a distinctive odour that we can focus on when we need to employ this technique - a bottle of perfume or a stick of chewing gum. The chewing gum will come in useful for the final step: taste. It does not matter what you use to engage the sense of taste but something pleasant will help to wind the exercise down calmly.

This technique is sensory focused to shift our attention away from the storm of internal thoughts and feelings of panic to the world outside ourselves. The technique conveys the message to our autonomic nervous system through all five senses that everything really is all right and it can switch off its emergency response.

> **"This technique is sensory focused to shift our attention away from the storm of internal thoughts"**

Sight

Sound

Taste

Touch

Smell

Breathe

Panic attacks produce hyperventilation. Hyperventilation floods our muscles with oxygen, making it ready to fight or to run away. But in a panic attack, there is nothing to run away from. Our deep brain is preparing us for a situation from our distant past, when what we are actually facing is the fear of giving a presentation or nerves before an exam. The situations that produce anxiety in the modern world are rarely resolved by fighting or running away.

One way to tell our amygdala that there really is nothing to worry about is to control the breath. By controlling our breathing we can nudge the brain and nervous system out of the flight/fight response. To do so, we need to change the breath pattern into an inbreath to a slow count of four and an outbreath to a slow count of four, preferably through the nose. It's important that the count is the same length for both.

At the start, when panic breathing has kicked in, it might be difficult to breathe through the nose but as soon as it is possible, we should switch to nose breathing. The difficulty with this technique is holding on to the slow, even breath count no matter what thoughts and feelings are assailing us, because it takes a little while for the message of slow,

"By controlling our breathing we can nudge the brain and nervous system out of the flight/fight response"

Repeat x 5

steady breathing to get through to the deep brain. But holding to slow, even breathing will send a message through the body to the deep brain: there is no emergency, switch off the danger hormones.

Note that some magazine articles advocate breathing out for twice as long as the inbreath, so an inbreath to the count of four and an outbreath to the count of eight. This rarely works as that breathing pattern works to put our system into its rest/digest state. Trying to switch immediately from the fight/flight response to rest/digest is simply too big a step - the body might panic even further at having these contradictory signals being sent to it. Using calm, slow breathing, with an even breath count puts us into a neutral physiological state, ready to respond to external stimuli. This allows the deep brain to reset itself and us to come out of the panic attack. The best way to prepare for dealing with a panic attack is to practise the long, 4/4 breath pattern beforehand, so that it has become grooved by repetition.

Progressive muscle relaxation

When we are anxious, our muscles tense. They do this because the deep brain is preparing the body for action, getting it ready to fight or run. However, people suffering from generalised anxiety disorder (GAD), the most common form of anxiety disorder, who live in a constant state of chronic anxiety, can have their muscles in a habitual, permanent state of tension. Progressive muscle relaxation is a way to systematically work through the muscle groups of the body, learning the difference between tension and relaxation, and discovering how to successively relax the muscles in one's body.

This is one technique that must be thoroughly practised, ideally twice a day at first. It takes about 15 minutes and you will need a room where you won't be disturbed. Start by lying on the ground or sitting comfortably in a chair. Take five long, slow even breaths.

Progressive muscle relaxation works by targeting muscle groups in turn. You first tense the muscle group as much as possible, for instance by squeezing your hand into the tightest fist you can manage. After five seconds, breathe out and relax those muscles. Concentrate on how the muscles feel when relaxed as opposed to when they are tense. You are learning what a relaxed muscle feels like.

People usually find it most effective working from feet to head or head to feet. We will look at feet to head but the sequence can be reversed. Some people find it helpful to have a recording to take them through the different muscle groups until they have learned them all.

Start by tensing one foot, curling the toes downwards. Hold, then relax, concentrating on the feel of a relaxed muscle. Then tighten the calf of the same leg by curling the toes upwards. Finish the leg by tensing the thigh muscles. Repeat on the other leg.

Clench one hand, then relax. Tense the whole arm by drawing your clenched fist to your shoulder. Repeat with the other arm.

Moving on to the trunk, start by tightening and then releasing the buttocks. Next, tense and relax your stomach. Tense the chest by taking and holding a really big breath, then breathe out.

To tense the neck and shoulders, hunch your shoulders towards your ears and then relax. Open the mouth as wide as it will go and then relax. Squish your eyes as tight shut as possible and then open them. Finally, tense your forehead by raising your eyebrows as high as you can, and then relax.

Once the exercise is familiar and you know what a relaxed muscle feels like, you might want to switch to tensing and releasing sections of the body together: both legs, torso, arms and neck, head. Finally, it may become possible to skip tensing completely and simply work through the body, relaxing each muscle group in turn.

The end result should be a relaxed body. As our brains work in partnership with our bodies, this will tell the brain that it can relax too.

> **"The end result should be a relaxed body and mind"**

Rainbow grounding

Rainbow grounding is a relaxation technique that works particularly well with anxious children. The pandemic and the government response to it produced major increases in anxiety among children so this might be a useful exercise to help an anxious child.

Again, it is based on moving attention out from the internal world to the world around us. Look around and try to see the rainbow in the colours of the things in your surroundings. Start with red, then move through the other colours, yellow, green, orange, purple and blue. It's probably best to skip indigo as most people are a bit vague as to how indigo differs from purple.

As you see each colour, really look at it to see what shade it is, its texture, the way the light falls upon it. It's perfectly all right to add non-rainbow colours to the list too, such as pink or black or grey or brown.

The best thing about this technique is its simplicity, which makes it particularly suitable for young children.

Memory games

The cycle of anxiety is perpetuated by distraction. Anxiety before writing an important essay can be relieved by looking at cat videos on YouTube, the instant release of tension brought through procrastination leading to a further deepening of the cycle.

However, there are times when feelings of anxiety can become so overwhelming that simply relieving them becomes more important than anything else. In these cases, effective and non-harmful distraction techniques can be both helpful and necessary.

Among the most effective of these are exercises that intensively use the most conscious part of our brains, the pre-frontal cortex. This is also the part of the brain that is most prone to worry, so finding something else for it to fixate upon can allow the rest of the brain to slowly relax.

Any mental exercise that is sufficiently demanding to require complete attention but is not too demanding to overtax a mind that is at its limits is ideal. Many people find memory games useful, whether that be reciting memorised poems or learning something new from scratch. Visual thinkers might try to remember and visualise something familiar: the kitchen worktop, the face of a loved one. More physical mental games, from jigsaws to Sudoku, can also be effective. However, as a general rule, high-intensity computer games should be avoided as these will increase stress levels.

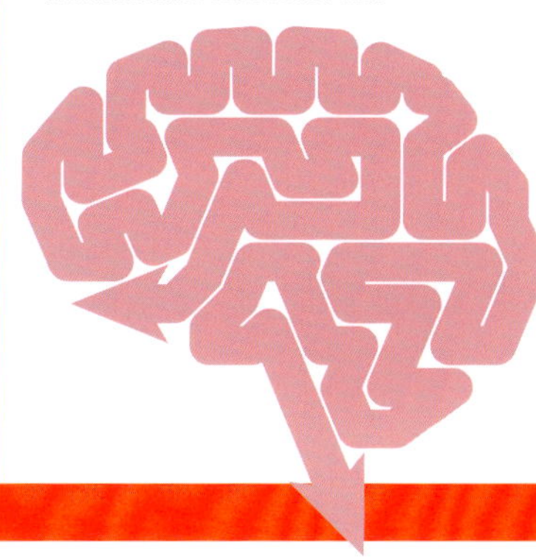

What is masking?

We explain what we mean by 'masking', what it looks like, and what the effects of masking can be

Words Julie Bassett

It's not always obvious that a person has ADHD. They may come across as organised, timely, calm and sociable, with no signs that would indicate any underlying struggles. However, what we see on the outside of a person is not always reflective of what's going on under the surface.

Many ADHD people 'mask' - they act or speak in a way considered socially acceptable to try and hide aspects of their life. Masking is a coping mechanism, an attempt to fit in with what is considered 'normal', but it can be disruptive and upsetting for a neurodivergent person to uphold long term.

You might mask a lot of the time and be very aware of it; or you might not recognise that what you're doing is masking; or maybe you're concerned that someone you care for is struggling with the impact of masking. We explain a little more about what this means and how it can affect you.

> **"There are lots of different ways in which a person with ADHD might mask"**

What does masking look like?

There are lots of different ways in which a person with ADHD might mask, depending on what symptoms they are trying to hide. Some people feel that they have to mask all the time; others only mask when they're in a specific situation, such as at work/school or when socialising.

This can mean hiding or managing physical behaviours. For example, it could be suppressing the urge to fidget, move around or exhibit stimming behaviours that you would usually do. This can be common among children at school who feel that they need to sit perfectly still so they don't get told off.

Masking can also mean putting in place excessive support tools to help you cope with daily life. This means things like creating lots of lists, writing down notes, settings reminders and timers, or creating other organisational systems that can take a lot of time to keep on top of but help you to outwardly seem in control. You might also do a lot of double-checking, such as checking you know where your belongings are or checking the time in the lead up to appointments, to ensure that you don't lose anything or end up being late.

Many people with ADHD overcompensate for their own perceived failures by working twice as hard to come across as capable and reliable. This can mean focusing intensely so as not to miss anything important, spending a lot of time on housework to keep up a clean and tidy environment, or taking on extra responsibilities to prove that you are able to do so.

Masking can also be avoidance of situations where you know you'd find it hard to cope, such as turning down social invitations, calling in sick to work or cancelling appointments.

The impact of masking

Putting all these masking techniques in place gives the impression of a person who's coping well with life - tidy home, never late, works hard. However, it's the effort of keeping all of this in place that's where the problem lies.

Holding in emotions because you are afraid of showing them can lead to internalising these feelings, which over time can increase the chance of mental health conditions, like depression. And trying to stay organised all the time with multiple systems in place is exhausting. It adds a lot more mental workload to

> "Masking can be avoidance of situations where you know you'd find it hard to cope"

your day than a neurotypical person has to manage, just to come across as what you perceive as 'normal'. It can lead to perfectionist tendencies and setting high expectations to try and prove to yourself, and those around you, that you can cope and that you're capable.

Masking symptoms day in, day out, can have serious consequences. For a start, masking is one reason why not everyone gets a timely diagnosis. If you're hiding the symptoms in an attempt to 'fit in', it might not be obvious how much you're struggling to cope with normal, daily activities. Sometimes, a person with ADHD doesn't know it themselves, as masking is ingrained in their lives, and they don't know that it isn't what everyone else is doing. It can also be harder to explain to people how much you're struggling when it doesn't show.

Over time, masking can contribute to ADHD burnout, which is a feeling of physical and mental exhaustion that comes from having to work so hard every day to keep plates spinning. Symptoms of burnout include fatigue, lack of motivation, feeling angry or irritable, feelings of sadness, withdrawing more from daily life and sleep struggles.

Spot the signs of masking

It might not always be obvious if someone is masking when they're around you. Spotting that someone is masking can help you to have a conversation about why they feel they need to mask and how you can help them to be more comfortable about unmasking.

Here are some signs to watch out for…

- A person is quiet or not contributing to conversation - they may be worried about saying the wrong thing, not knowing when to speak or be concerned about interrupting.
- A person has a lot of lists, timers or routines - this can be a way of staying on top of normal daily activities.
- A person may mirror your actions - this can be a way of learning how to act or speak in a certain situation.
- A person might seem tense or agitated - this can be because of hidden anxiety and stress about an upcoming task or appointment.
- A person might seem very focused on you when you're talking - this could be because they are worried about losing track of the conversation.

If you're concerned that someone is masking regularly, let them know that it's okay to let their guard down around you. This can come as a relief, giving someone a chance to be themselves without any pressure.

Taking the pressure off

If you notice that you're masking, or that someone you care about is masking (see the boxout for signs to watch out for), it can be hard to learn how to unmask. Masking can become so much a part of us that we don't know where the mask ends.

It's best to start with the masking behaviours that cause you the most distress. For example, you might find that having lots of organisational systems in place is more positive than not and enables you to have a strong routine. But you might also find that holding in thoughts and emotions is making you feel unheard and lonely. In this case, you could start with learning how to face and express emotions, whether that's by talking to someone you trust or by seeking support from a therapist.

It can be a good idea to connect with local support services so that you can meet other people in the same situation. There might be groups that you can attend, which can be useful, or sharing ideas and building tools to make daily life easier. It's best to address one mask at a time, or it can be an overwhelming process.

A lot of the unmasking process, however, comes down to working on your own self-esteem and self-confidence; learning who you are as a person and accepting your behaviours and thoughts as part of your unique self. Acceptance can be a powerful tool, and embracing who you are can empower you to thrive in your life, rather than suffer through it.

Does my child have ADHD?

How does neurodiversity manifest itself in children, and is it something to worry about? We speak to Dr Sinead Doyle to understand what ADHD and autism mean, and how the UK's doctors treat neurodiversity

Words Ben Grafton

Dr Sinead Doyle

Consultant Community Paediatrician

Dr Sinead Doyle is a Consultant Community Paediatrician in the UK, specialising in the care of children with emotional and learning difficulties. During her career she has worked with children who live with neurodiversities and mental health conditions.

What exactly do we mean by 'neurodiversity' in children?

Neurodiversity is a broad umbrella term that describes the variety of ways in which our brains can function and process information as human beings. It is generally a positive term which celebrates our differences and the benefits that neurodiversity can bring both to individuals and to society as a whole.

Neurodiversity is generally thought to include a number of conditions including Autism Spectrum Disorder (ASD), Attention Deficit and Hyperactivity Disorder (ADHD), Developmental Coordination Disorder (DCD - previously termed dyspraxia) and specific learning difficulties, including dyslexia (difficulties with reading and writing) or dyscalculia (difficulties with processing numbers and arithmetic). In some definitions, mental and emotional health difficulties may also fall within the scope of this umbrella term. These conditions can all be diagnosed at any stage

A

of life; however, due to increased awareness of how these conditions present, as well as availability of diagnostic and support services, they are increasingly being diagnosed in childhood.

What are some of the more common conditions that we might see in children who may fall under this umbrella term?

Currently, the most commonly diagnosed of these conditions in children are autism and ADHD. Diagnostic services for children have seen a huge increase in referrals over the last decade, alongside an increase in private diagnostic services due to long waiting times for assessment through the NHS. Autism and ADHD present differently, however, it is recognised that there is an overlap between these two conditions, with some children and young people meeting the criteria for both conditions.

Autism is defined as a 'social communication disorder' with the key feature being difficulties with social interaction. This can present as anxiety in social situations, difficulties navigating friendships and relationships, and difficulties understanding both social 'rules' (how we are expected to behave in 'polite' society) and social 'cues' (that is, how we communicate our thoughts or feelings through eye contact, gesture and tone of voice for example).

Other key features include a strong need for routine or order; in younger children this may be seen during play, when they may demonstrate a reduced range of interests, difficulties with flexibility or taking turns, and a preference for more structured and less imaginative play.

Some children and young people will present with what are termed 'sensory processing difficulties' – these are differences in the way they process information obtained through our five senses (that is touch, taste, smell, sound or visual stimuli). If children experience sensory input in a more heightened way, they may look to dampen this by covering their ears with loud noises, for example, or choosing to eat blander foods. Equally, if they have a reduced experience of sensory input, they may seek to increase this by choosing toys with bright lights or by performing large movements of their body.

In comparison, ADHD is a condition defined by significant difficulties with maintaining attention and focus, managing impulse control and managing excess levels of energy. As with autism, to make a diagnosis, there must be evidence that the child or young person's symptoms are leading to a significant impairment in their life, both at home and in the educational setting. As both conditions are related to brain development in early life (also known as 'neurodevelopmental' conditions), there must also be evidence of symptoms being present or developing in early childhood.

Is it important to seek a diagnosis if you feel that your child is presenting with one of these conditions?

Seeking a diagnosis can be a long journey for some families, and some parents may be concerned about seeking a 'label' for their child, and what that might mean for them in the future. However, if the child or young person is struggling because of their difficulties with learning and

> “A diagnosis may offer them a better understanding of their identity”

taking part in school, for example, receiving a diagnosis may allow them to obtain additional support in school and from other support groups and charities.

They may also receive support from health professionals where needed, and in some cases medication may be offered to support specific symptoms. For the young people themselves, a diagnosis may offer them a better understanding of their identity and give a sense of belonging. There is evidence that an earlier diagnosis leads to better long-term outcomes, particularly in terms of emotional wellbeing and mental health.

In general, it is felt that a diagnosis should offer some benefit to the child or young person. If a child is demonstrating some features of a neurodevelopmental condition but is otherwise thriving, it may be worth their parents discussing with the school or family practitioner about whether a referral to a diagnostic service would be beneficial.

So how exactly can these conditions impact a child within their home and school life?

Every child presents differently and will face varying degrees and types of difficulties. In addition, a child's difficulties will always be considered within the context of their family as a whole.

If we consider a child with autism, one of the most common challenges that they might face is developing friendships and social relationships, particularly within the school setting, and some children may need significant levels of support with this. They may also find the school environment challenging due to their sensory processing needs, and adaptations may need to be made to the learning environment. For some children, there may be additional difficulties with development of verbal communication and with their learning; this will require support from other professionals such as speech and language therapists and educational psychologists. In some cases, the child's learning needs may be better met in a specialist educational setting.

For children with ADHD, learning can also be impacted, although this is often secondary to difficulties with focusing and sitting still. Children can struggle to listen and follow instructions, and can become frustrated easily, leading to conflict with other children in the class and what appear to be on the surface 'behavioural difficulties'. Sensory processing needs are also a part of this condition and need to be supported accordingly in the learning setting.

Having a child with autism or ADHD can have a significant impact on family life. Due to their sensory processing needs, the child may require additional support with self-care, including toileting, washing, dressing and maintaining a healthy diet. Family life may also need to be adapted; attending social gatherings may require planning and support, and many families find certain activities may need to be avoided altogether. Behavioural challenges are often seen at home, which will have an impact not only on the parents but also the siblings.

Do these conditions always present in early childhood?

A key feature of autism is that it is a spectrum, so some children will present at a very young age, while others may not present until they are teenagers or indeed young adults, when social demands have increased. Children who have developed good speech and learning skills are likely to present later than those with difficulties in these areas. This is partly due to the fact that children with good learning can learn to adapt in social settings (sometimes termed 'masking'). Having said this, increased awareness of these conditions does mean that young people are now being diagnosed both with autism and ADHD at an earlier age. It is important to mention that how children present can differ between boys and girls; historically boys presented with more classic symptoms so that girls often slipped under the radar until much later.

As a medical professional, how do you care for children with these conditions?

One of the key roles of medical professionals is to provide a robust and thorough diagnostic assessment. This is supported by guidance from 'NICE' - the National Institute for Clinical Evidence, which advises how these assessments should be performed. One key feature is that they should be multidisciplinary - and so we will work alongside other professionals such as speech and language therapists or clinical psychologists to assess and give a diagnosis.

The assessment process itself has a number of stages - it may look slightly different in different centres, but will typically consist of an information-gathering appointment and an assessment with the child, either in their school or at the assessment centre. Sometimes written information may also be requested from the school or other professionals involved in the child's care. Getting the diagnosis right is important and so the process can feel quite drawn out for families at times. Other developmental or mental health difficulties must be considered and excluded, and the child must meet specific criteria set out in the International Classification of Diseases (ICD-version 11).

> "Getting the diagnosis right is important and so the process can feel quite drawn out"

Once we've clarified whether or not a child meets the criteria for a diagnosis, we then consider the support that child might need. Some children and families may require practical support, for example with eating, growth or toileting. Sleep can also be an area of difficulty and families can be referred to specialist sleep services for support. Other allied health professionals may become involved where needed, such as dieticians or occupational therapists (who support with sensory processing needs). Other families may need support around behaviour or emotional needs and they will be sign posted to appropriate services.

As medical professionals, we do liaise closely with education to ensure a child's needs are being met in school. If a child's needs are felt to warrant an Education Health and Care Plan (EHCP - previously called a 'statement of educational needs'), we will provide a medical report towards this.

What's the best way for parents and family to support their child?

If you are concerned about your child, raise these concerns early with professionals who can help - I would recommend approaching the school SENCO (special educational needs co-ordinator) if your child is of school age, or the health visitor if your child is pre-school age. They will be able to discuss these concerns with you and discuss referral processes and appropriate support services available.

If you are concerned that your child requires further support in school, it is again a good idea to discuss this with the SENCO. Both schools and parents are able to apply for an Education Health and Care Plan if a child needs a certain level of support. An assessment is performed, and a document created which outlines the support the child requires - this is also supported by additional funding for that child.

If you are concerned that your child is not placed in an appropriate educational setting and would like support, you can contact the SENDIAS team (Special Educational Needs and Disability Information, Advice and Support) within your local area.

What about the emotional support of families?

Families may want to reach out to appropriate charities who can offer excellent support, including support from families going through similar experiences. These may include UK-wide charities such as the National Autistic Society or the ADHD Foundation, or local charities supporting families in the region. Details of these are usually found through the Local Offer - a page on your local council website with listings of specific support groups in your area.

If there are specific challenges at home, families can self-refer to a team within the council termed Early Help - they will perform an assessment and if applicable will allocate a family support worker. Self-referral can be made through Early Help Hubs in the local area.

If you are concerned about you or your child's emotional or mental health, you can approach your GP or the school nursing team for details of support services available. You may also want to look at charities such as Mind (www.mind.org.uk) or Young Minds (www.youngminds.org.uk)

Why might someone choose not to get a diagnosis?

I can't speak for individuals who have been through the diagnostic process but I can imagine that it may seem like a daunting process, as it often involves numerous different professionals and multiple appointments. If you struggle in unfamiliar social settings or around unfamiliar people then coming to an assessment centre may seem overwhelming. If you are concerned, it may be worth speaking to the centre to consider ways that the assessment can be modified to support you.

As mentioned previously, some people may be fearful of receiving a diagnosis that may be seen as a 'label' or associated with perceived stigma. Fortunately, the awareness around neurodiversity has much improved and inclusion and support is now greatly encouraged. Many young people often feel relief and improved self-esteem after receiving a diagnosis.

For some young people or families, they may recognise certain traits of these conditions but not feel any need for a diagnosis as the young person is thriving and does not require support. There may also not be enough features for that person to receive a diagnosis, which is perfectly acceptable - I think we can all at times empathise with a certain need for self-isolation and a sense of control!

The key is to recognise children who will benefit from a diagnosis and who require additional support to ensure they thrive as they transition to adulthood.

Supporting your child

Failing to recognise symptoms of ADHD can lead to children struggling academically and socially, so it's important for parents to arm themselves with the facts

Words Ben Grafton

To a 1990s school child, classmates with ADHD were generally considered to be those bouncing around the walls and chattering in your ear while you tried to solve your algebra equations. There was little known about this condition save for the fact that classmates who had been diagnosed with it often found themselves studying alone, with one-to-one support, or given mysterious medication. If you were a high academic achiever, there was no way that you, your teachers or your parents would ever have considered the possibility of ADHD, even if some of the early warning signs were beginning to present themselves.

Fast forward three decades and as a global society we are in a much savvier place in terms of understanding neurodiversity and the common neurodevelopmental disorder of ADHD. The condition is no longer the preserve of the hyperactive boy procrastinators, unable to sit still long enough to complete the history test. Greater understanding of the subtypes of ADHD, together with better awareness of early warning signs, means that children now have much greater access to support services. Accessing this support is crucial in terms of ensuring a successful pathway through their academic and social lives.

How ADHD affects children

The UK's National Institute for Health and Care Excellence (NICE) estimates that the percentage of children with ADHD globally is around 5% (not taking into account those waiting for assessments). ADHD is a common neurodevelopmental impairment of the brain's executive functions, which in children and young people manifests as an inability to control impulses, concentrate, be organised and in some cases, have difficulty staying sedate for prolonged periods. Despite common misconceptions, ADHD is not 'bad behaviour' or a sign of bad parenting. Rather, ADHD is a condition that is related to how the brain is 'wired' to self-regulate and process information.

There are three recognised subgroups of ADHD - hyperactive, inattentive and combined. For a formal diagnosis of ADHD, children generally need to present with multiple symptoms before the age of 12 years. In the UK, a child would need to present with six or more of the recognised symptoms for over six months duration; these symptoms would also need to be present in multiple settings, such as home and school. During the assessment process, the assessing professional will also look for evidence that the child's symptoms are having a

> "The reality is that ADHD can present in many ways and can affect boys and girls differently"

significant detrimental impact at home and at school.

It is important to remember that a child's brain development is a continuous process; therefore for most children a healthy dose of love, patience and understanding from caregivers, bolstered by practical support, will lead to positive academic and social growth.

In times gone by, parents and teachers might have dismissed any problematic behaviour as 'growing pains' or a need to 'knuckle down'. But today we are moving forward as a society towards a greater understanding of each of our neurotypes, and with it a desire to optimise how our brain works, in order to live the life that we want to lead rather than the one we might feel condemned to live.

Ignore stereotypes

While the stereotype of the overactive boy charging around the classroom is based in some truth (the ratio of boys to girls with ADHD is three-to-one according to the National Institute for Health in the US), the reality is that ADHD can present in many ways and can affect boys and girls differently.

For example, hyperactivity may present differently in boys than girls, who may resist the urge to run around but instead might display verbose tendencies or impatience. Since girls have a higher propensity towards the inattentive subgroup of ADHD, their struggle to concentrate is not as disruptive, and can therefore pass below the radar of teachers and family.

What to look out for

Symptoms of the hyperactive subgroup include: constant fidgeting or tapping of hands or feet; running about or climbing in situations where

this is not expected behaviour; difficulty staying quiet; talking excessively and being constantly 'on the go'; completing people's sentences and not waiting your turn.

Symptoms of the inattentive subgroup in children might include making careless mistakes in schoolwork; having difficulty sustaining attention in tasks or play; difficulty listening to a teacher's instructions, organising tasks and activities; becoming bored easily; losing belongings frequently; and being easily distracted and forgetful.

What might ADHD mean for my child?

Difficulties with completing conventional assessments can lead to the education system underestimating a child's academic ability. Pupils may also miss key information during lessons and struggle to complete work, which can further hamper their academic progress.

The social, emotional and mental health outcomes for those with ADHD are also stark if the condition is left unaddressed. ADHD may impact a child's ability to sustain healthy and appropriate social interactions and friendships, and conflicts with peers can be common.

The ADHD Foundation highlights that rates of anxiety, depression, self-harm and criminality are all elevated among those with ADHD, while increased risk of financial worries and unstable employment mean it is important to get on top of it as early as possible.

However, it's not all negative. According to a 2017 study published by the National Institute of Health, children with ADHD demonstrated high levels of empathy and emotional understanding alongside skills in maths and logic. Those with ADHD can also be 'out of the box' thinkers and creative problem-solvers, a trait that is highly sought after in the creative industries.

Overcoming society's stigma

The stigma associated with ADHD - and neurodivergence in general - is a barrier that must be overcome in order for children to access the full range of support networks available to them. Parents in denial about the level of support their child requires often has its roots in a shame and blame culture. Just as pervasive is the fear of being 'that parent', the one who is thought to be label-seeking. This can prevent parents from acting

Sleeping tips

According to the UK's National Health Service, it is estimated that people with ADHD are at least 50% more likely to experience sleeping problems, and this is especially heightened during adolescence. There are several steps that those with ADHD can take to optimise sleep. The first thing is to create an appropriate environment: quiet and comfortable rooms work for most people, while noise-cancelling earphones, eye masks, ear plugs, blackout curtains, or a white noise machine can also help. Avoiding activities before bed that require brain alertness is a must, so minimising screen time and video games is necessary. Develop sleep rituals and consistent sleep patterns so that your body knows it is winding down to sleep. This could be listening to calming music, reading or listening to an audio book, having a hot bath or shower, stretching, yoga or deep breathing, all of which reduce stress and anxiety. If you are worried about what you need to achieve, make your to-do lists and schedules to organise the tasks. And while exercise is positive for those with ADHD, doing so before sleep can be detrimental, while caffeine before bed should also be avoided.

on their intuition in instances when they know their child would benefit from support.

Empathy from caregivers and teachers is a vital part of supporting a child with ADHD in an education system that still privileges 'neurotypical' brains. Assessments within the current educational system inevitably require skills in concentration, memory, organisation and the ability to follow multi-step instructions. Meanwhile impulsive behaviour, which disrupts the teacher and the classroom, can lead to punitive action, which in turn impacts on a child's self-esteem and can lead to feelings of anxiety. A sense of feeling misunderstood may also have far-reaching consequences in later life.

Supporting children at home

Children will require ongoing support at home, both with their organisational and attention difficulties, and also with emotional regulation, which may present as difficult or challenging behaviours.

In the early years, play is an important tool to hone skills such as turn-taking and listening. It can also help children understand their emotions and how to regulate them, and it supports the development of desirable social behaviour.

As children get older, the use of firm boundaries and structure allows for a fallback plan when emotions are high, while a fixed routine takes the pressure off the child to remember things. Listening skills and non-verbal communication should continue to be encouraged, so social relationships develop positively alongside the child's self-esteem and confidence.

For teenagers, there might be a need for frequent check-ins on their stress or tiredness levels, without saturating them with too many questions. Speaking to a teenager like a young adult and explaining when you are feeling tired and stressed, could encourage them to express their needs, such as for space and alone time. This two-way communication channel can in turn boost their confidence to articulate their emotions when struggling under the weight of their symptoms. In all cases, praising children and young people, celebrating them, encouraging them to step out of their comfort zones, and rewarding even small steps towards progress, goes a long way to helping them develop social skills and self-confidence.

Things to avoid

Avoid direct confrontation or attempting to reason with your child's impulsive behaviour, which is often

> "Presenting options enables a child with ADHD to feel as though they have some control"

counterproductive. Do not use 'you' language, which can be interpreted as accusatory. Instead, communicate clear facts to them about how things have impacted you or others.

Presenting options and choices enables a child with ADHD to feel as though they have some control in a world that does not always make them feel like they have any, allowing them to minimise exposure to trigger situations. Discipline can be maintained thanks to a pre-established framework of rules and consequences. This means that, while it is your choice whether to punish minor rule breaking, there is a strategy in place at all times for inappropriate behaviour. In short, their ADHD is never a get out of jail free card.

Ways to support a child with ADHD at school

There are a number of ways young children who have ADHD can be supported in the classroom, but no one-strategy-fits-all. The room setup can be helpful from the get-go: the teacher can arrange the desks in a way that supports a pupil's learning while minimising disruption to other pupils. An ideal layout is to place pupils with ADHD front and centre, away from windows, sat close to positive role models and a suitable distance from other desks to minimise temptation for distraction.

Regularly giving pupils breaks, with tasks broken down into manageable chunks enables children to progress, while repeating instructions and supplying them both verbally and visually means a student feels confident they are on the right track towards progress. Activities should vary - they should be practical, interactive and theoretical so as not to heap too much pressure on the child's concentration spans.

Children with ADHD often respond well to reward systems, so giving regular positive feedback for achievements is beneficial. Celebrating and supporting the uniqueness of a child's strengths can go a long way to contributing to a positive educational experience. More recent common developments, such as the use of standing desks and the use of fidget toys in class, can also aid focus dramatically.

For the more disruptive pupils, behavioural management techniques, such as formulating agreements of behaviour with the pupil as a form of 'contract', allows for a negotiation and recognition of inappropriate behaviour, while time-outs are also efficient ways to break from the

Reading tips

Reading enables a child to experience the sensation of learning on their own. Being engrossed in a story might encourage your child to hyper-focus – a useful trait of ADHD – while focused reading is a skill that will be essential in their education and professional lives beyond. In many cases it is best to encourage 'reading for pleasure' as opposed to enforced reading that might come, say, in the form of homework. If reading forms part of a bedtime routine, or a regular afternoon activity, this will also help the child to look forward to it, giving them the dopamine that their brain may crave. As an alternative, audio books might provide greater and more inclusive engagement, especially when paired with regular movement, such as standing or gentle bouncing on an exercise ball.

In daylight hours, walks in the park or simply moving around a bedroom can help a child focus, and while encouragement towards appropriate movement in social settings is desirable, movement in general shouldn't be impeded or punished as this can contribute to a child's feelings of shame or alienation. The environment where a child reads is important: it should be in a calm space and away from distractions.

repetitiveness of the classroom. Co-operative and goal-oriented work can be useful for pupils who seem disengaged or withdrawn. In terms of organisation, the structure introduced at home can be supported by routine and weekly timetables at school, in addition to mnemonic devices, such as flashcards, folders, and colour-coded paperwork.

Further and higher education

Individual student support workers for taking notes, printouts on coloured paper and extra time allocated for assignments and examinations, are all considered reasonable adjustments for students with ADHD today. It's recommended that students read lecture notes or presentation slides in advance of the class if possible, and to have them open on a screen to aid processing. They might also be permitted to record an audio file of classes. Students should make use of individual tutorials to ensure they have fully understood the previous week's work, and to communicate learning needs to course faculty members as they arise.

During lectures and seminars, students with ADHD might want to reduce as many distractions as possible, by sitting at the front of the class and away from windows. The ADHD Foundation in the UK recommends adopting 'active listening techniques'. These are things like asking a question if you feel your mind wandering, or making notes immediately, as this will help to re-engage your focus on the lecture. It also recommends keeping hydrated throughout the day, which aids concentration.

For revision, technology is a brilliant way to support neurodivergent learning. Tablets and electronic notebooks host apps that have been designed to support those who struggle to organise themselves, and can be a useful way of keeping on top of a mounting academic to-do list. Speech-to-text, timers and apps that limit social media consumption can all be implemented with great results.

Effective home lifestyle changes

It is perhaps no surprise that good sleep, a balanced, nutritional diet and exercise can all help to reduce the effect of the symptoms associated with ADHD. Common sense approaches to caffeine and screen time are advised. Nutrition forms part of a multi-dimensional approach to managing ADHD, and sits alongside medicinal, behavioural therapy, educational adjustments and coaching from mentors and family. Mindfulness, while not altering the brain's

development, can also help children to address the difficulties associated with their impulsive behaviour.

Consistent timings for bedtime, mealtimes, homework and chores are key, and encouraging children to take part in hobbies in which they excel supports their self-esteem. Family, such as siblings and grandparents, can of course provide extra support, but need to be kept informed of the strategies you are embracing in order for them to best contribute to the happy and healthy development of your child.

A holistic approach

Many adults wish they'd had a greater understanding of their neurotype. To them, life might have felt like going on a cruise with the ship's wheel and rudder in imperfect harmony. As a result we want the next generation of children to be in the best possible place to be able to make decisions regarding their lives without working against their brain's frustrating tendencies. That's why a joined-up approach that sees caregivers, parents and schools working hand-in-hand with general practitioners, paediatricians and medical experts, all of whom keep in regular communication, can allow ADHD-diagnosed young people to thrive academically and socially.

"Nutrition forms part of a multi-dimensional approach to managing ADHD"

For families where two parents are present, working together will reap rewards. Doing your own research is recommended but also try to recognise when your deep-dive into ADHD is proving damaging into your own wellbeing. Waiting lists for diagnoses are long and the amount of undiagnosed children with ADHD worldwide potentially reaches into the millions. The balance between wanting a diagnosis and allowing children the necessary time and space to make mistakes and learn, is a delicate one. Listen to your parental instincts but ask yourself what is the benefit of a diagnosis. If your child has received an ADHD diagnosis, you did not make a mistake. On the contrary - for your commitment to your child's wellbeing, you should be commended.

Sticks and stones

While we may be aware of the impact that bullying has on children, too often we ignore the scarred adults it leaves in its wake

Words Emma Green

Bullying is generally seen as a childhood rite of passage, something most of us will go through at some stage in our development but from which we will usually emerge unscathed, or at least, a little bit tougher and a little more humbled. But what happens when this isn't the case? While school may seem a fleeting memory to some, for others, it is the catalyst for deep psychological wounds that refuse to heal, even decades on.

Research into bullying first began in the 1970s, and while there are no official statistics on the prevalence of bullying in schools, studies have suggested that more than half of all young people will experience some kind of peer victimisation in their lifetime. The UK's Department for Education defines bullying as behaviour by an individual or group, repeated over time, that intentionally hurts another individual or group, either physically or emotionally. Although bullying can take many forms, experiences tend to differ across genders. Numerous studies have shown that boys are more inclined to be involved in physical attacks while girls are more likely to be affected by emotional forms of bullying, such as verbal abuse and social exclusion.

While anyone can be a victim of bullying, some demographics are more prone to experience it than others. In particular, neurodiverse people face a higher risk of being bullied by their peers. Neurodiverse pupils are twice as likely to be bullied than their neurotypical counterparts, and those with autism are at the highest risk out of everyone to be targeted by bullies.

Why do people bully?

The most predominant factor in why someone might be bullied is simply for just being 'different'. Dr Ellen deLara, an associate professor of social work at Syracuse University and author of *Bullying Scars: The Impact on Adult Life and Relationships*, explains that "being different in any way is the main reason that a child is selected for mistreatment. Adolescents prize conformity and therefore will bully someone who looks or behaves outside the norm."

She suggests that bullying is used as a mechanism to put anyone who is deemed different "outside of the herd" in order to correct this discrepancy. Trivial perceived differences in someone's height, weight, appearance, hair colour, disposition, class or intelligence, could be the very incentive for subjecting them to peer-on-peer abuse.

Dr Sheri Bauman, a leading academic in bullying prevention and a professor of counselling at the University of Arizona, believes that social status is at the core of most bullying.

"Bullies are trying to get or maintain status," she explains. "If they have it, they want to keep it; if they don't, they want to get it." Dr Bauman says that most bullying peaks around early adolescence, just as children are moving on to secondary education.

"Bullying goes way up then because the new school is bigger and there's more competition," she says. "It makes sense if you think of the bully as needing admiration, power and status. Bullying is a way of getting that."

Despite zero-tolerance policies in schools and the threat of punishment, bullying can seem impossible to contain for educators.

"For the bully, it's very rewarding," explains Dr Bauman. "Bullies get all these rewards for behaving badly, so it becomes very difficult to encourage them to change their behaviour."

When speaking to former bullies, Dr deLara also spotted another pattern. "Most of them said they didn't think they were bullying," she says. "They were just teasing or fooling around and didn't think the other person was upset by it. It's not even a rationale. It's exactly how they think."

Long-term effects on victims

For the victims, the aftermath of being bullied as a child can linger far beyond the schoolyard. Research carried out by the University of Warwick shows that childhood bullying can 'cast a shadow over the whole life course, leading to serious illness, poor social relationships and problems holding down a regular job'. Further studies have also shown that being a victim of bullying is associated with increased mental and physical health problems, along with lower academic attainment and income, even after accounting for other contributing factors such as family hardship.

Repeated exposure to abuse as a child can also change the brain. Verbal bullying, particularly in early adolescence, can damage or hinder development in key structures of the brain including areas that process emotions and control behaviour. This could partially explain why individuals who were bullied as children are more prone to experiencing long-term psychological conditions such as anxiety, depression and post-traumatic stress disorder (PTSD).

Safeguarding children from bullying

It can be incredibly hard as parents to have to witness your child being bullied, but it can be even harder to know exactly what to do to get them through it. Fortunately, there are some protective factors that we can put in place to insulate children from becoming damaged adults later on in life. First and foremost is fostering a supportive family environment where open communication is encouraged so the child feels secure enough to disclose what is happening to them. Additionally, attending therapy or a bullying support group will help children practise their social skills within a safe space. Encouraging positive friendships is also important, as peer support can be a powerful protector against the negative impacts of bullying. Enrolling children in activities that give them a sense of purpose and where they can meet like-minded children can help to counter some of the rejection and exclusion they may face at school.

Adult Post-Bullying Syndrome

While conducting research for her book, Dr deLara interviewed more than 800 people about their experiences of bullying in their formative years. She discovered a trend in symptoms exhibited amongst those who'd been severely bullied as children that she refers to as 'Adult Post-Bullying Syndrome' (APBS). Although some symptoms share similarities with cases of complex PTSD, the term 'Adult Post-Bullying Syndrome' encapsulates the unique set of psychological, emotional and social challenges that former victims of bullying continue to grapple with well into adulthood.

Whereas not everyone who is bullied as a child will experience trauma, many victims will display some, if not all, the signs of APBS. One of these symptoms is issues with self-esteem and shame.

"Children who are victims of bullying and harassment are made to feel ashamed of who they are," writes Dr. deLara. "They feel ashamed, hurt and confused when they are shunned by their peers. They feel ashamed that they are singled out for taunting, and they feel ashamed and angry that they cannot figure out how to make it stop."

Bullying can profoundly impact one's sense of self-worth and identity, leading to negative self-perceptions and diminished confidence.

> **"Bullying can profoundly impact one's sense of self-worth and identity, leading to negative self-perceptions"**

Some may try to overcompensate for feelings of shame by becoming people pleasers, another symptom of APBS. Dr deLara believes that the driving force behind this behaviour is that "if you can figure out how to be everything and do everything right, then nothing bad will happen to you, which of course, is impossible." Approval-seeking and trying to be perfect becomes a people pleaser's best form of protection from future criticism and harassment, but it only serves to further erode their sense of self and to be a passive participant in their interpersonal relationships.

For others, the shame that resides within them is expressed through feelings of anger, rage and revenge - another sign of APBS - and they may try to channel this aggression through revenge fantasies. This could manifest in a relentless drive to surpass those who bullied them and through constant monitoring of social media as a gauge to see whether they're doing 'better' than their former bullies. In extreme cases, this thirst for revenge can result in acts of violence such as school shootings.

Suffering from emotional problems and psychiatric disorders later in life are a key characteristic of APBS, particularly depression and anxiety. Another is a propensity towards substance misuse which may come in the form of food, alcohol or drugs. This is used as a maladaptive coping mechanism to alleviate emotional pain and distress, but can further exacerbate mental health problems as well as negatively impact relationships and employment prospects. Furthermore, adults with APBS also tend to have issues with body image, particularly those who were overweight as a child; a remnant carried over into adulthood from past ridicule and disparagement about their appearance.

The heinous treatment that victims of bullying have to suffer at the hands of their peers means that it can be very hard for them to trust others, especially those who resemble their former bullies in some way.

"Many people develop a prejudice based on the type of person who bullied them," says Dr deLara. "For example, sometimes people will say to me, 'I hate athletes', while others say that being bullied made them hate people in general."

This lack of trust in others can have a knock-on effect on a victim's ability to form and maintain healthy relationships later in life. Their fear of rejection, betrayal or abandonment learned early on in childhood can impede their ability to connect with others authentically, leading to social withdrawal and isolation. Even if they can establish connections with others, the effects of bullying can spill over into their adult relationships, contributing to difficulties in communication, intimacy and setting boundaries with their romantic partners, friends, family members and colleagues. Problems in relationships and trusting others are two more classic signs of APBS.

Moving beyond the trauma

While the impact of childhood bullying can be devastating, it is not inevitable. With the right support, victims of bullying can heal from the trauma of their past and go on to build fulfilling lives. Therapy can help to rebuild self-esteem, create a positive sense of identity, develop healthy coping mechanisms and cultivate better relationships. It does this by challenging negative beliefs that may have been internalised from being bullied, as well as helping an individual to practise forgiveness, advocate for themselves and to assert healthy boundaries. Cognitive behavioural therapy (CBT), trauma-informed therapy and eye movement desensitization and reprocessing (EMDR) therapy are all effective methods for exploring and processing past experiences of bullying. Seeking professional support can also help to treat any additional psychiatric disorders that may have developed as a result of being bullied, while simultaneously addressing the root cause of the trauma.

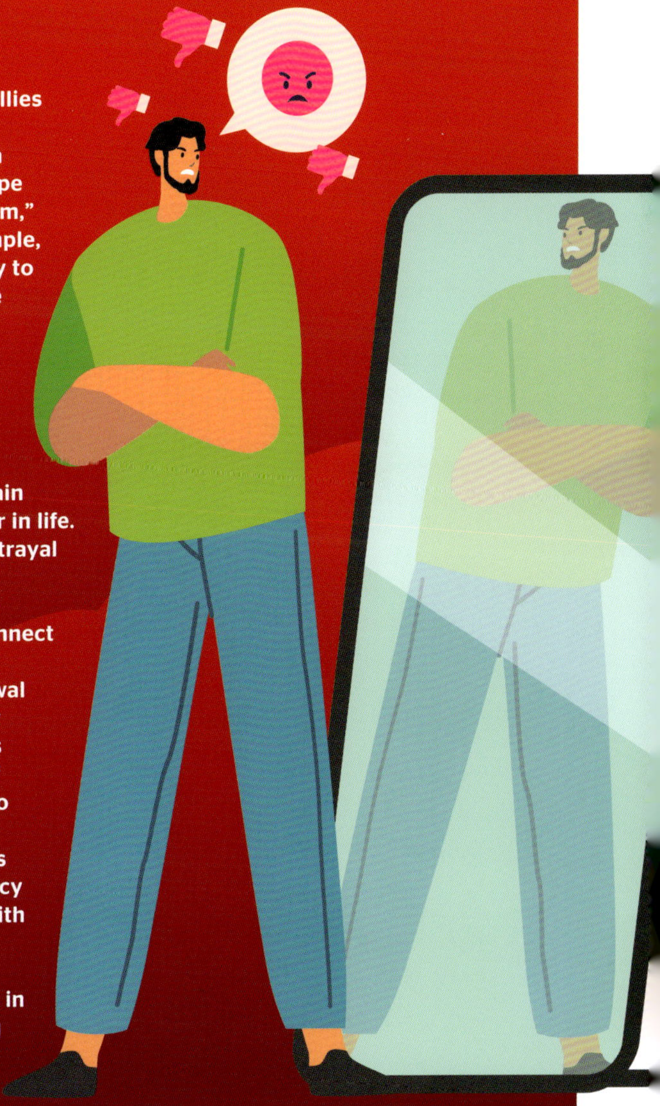

Post-traumatic growth

During her research, Dr deLara discovered an additional and surprising symptom of APBS.

"I didn't expect anybody to tell me that there would be anything positive [to come out of being bullied]," she says. "When I asked adolescents, they said 'absolutely not'. But when I talked to adults, 47% of them said that being bullied had had a positive effect on them."

These positive effects can manifest in various ways from an increased sense of empathy and an enhanced moral consciousness to more self-sufficiency and less dependence on others. It could also result in a stronger push towards goal attainment and success, as a way of proving themselves. This form of 'post-traumatic growth' arises from how individuals choose to respond and cope with their trauma, which may never have come to the fore if it hadn't been for being a victim of bullying. However, Dr deLara emphasises that although there may be positive outcomes for some, the negative effects associated with peer-on-peer abuse far outweigh the positives and should never be used as an excuse to endorse bullying.

Long-term effects on bullies

Surprisingly, it's not just the victims themselves who suffer because of bullying. Research has shown that those who were bullies in school are also more likely to be affected by lifelong problems. In 2019, the Scottish Centre for Youth and Criminal Justice published a report on bullying behaviours. It states that children who were perpetrators of bullying between the ages of seven and 12 were significantly more likely to be arrested by the age of 30. Moreover, the odds of frequent bullies having committed more than five crimes by the age of 26 was almost seven times more likely than those who didn't bully. Another report commissioned for NHS Scotland on addressing school violence and bullying found that young people who displayed bullying behaviours were at increased risk of depression and suicidal thoughts, as well as being more likely to drop out of school and be involved in criminal acts.

> "The effects of bullying can spill over into relationships"

'Just get over it'

If we know that there are such dire and pervasive consequences for everyone involved in bullying, why is it an area of research so often overlooked by academics?

"It's a very difficult kind of research to do," explains Dr Bauman. "The gold standard is to study a group of kids and then follow them into adulthood. But it's very challenging because people move or die or decide they don't want to participate anymore. It's also very expensive and hard to get funding for these types of long-term, prospective studies."

Dr deLara also believes that the lack of research is fuelled by society's ignorance of how enduring the effects of childhood bullying can be.

"As a culture, we say, 'This is childhood, that's over, now you're an adult'," she says. "The minute you leave school, people think that's the end of that and you should be over it."

It's easy to see how this thought process has infiltrated our collective mind. Old adages such as 'Sticks and stones may break my bones but words shall never hurt me' and 'What doesn't kill you, makes you stronger' are drummed into us from an early age to bolster our resilience towards interpersonal cruelty. Although these proverbs are relatively harmless, they also serve to deflect and minimise the impact that words and negative treatment by our peers can have on us. Until, as a society, we start to take the effects of childhood bullying more seriously, we will continue to see them play out in traumatised adults long after the echoes of the school bell have ceased.

Don't suffer in silence

Talking to someone about being bullied might feel almost as tough as dealing with the bullying itself, but it's essential.

Even if you feel it will be upsetting or embarrassing, don't let that, or any threats about speaking out, stop you.

Who you tell will depend on who you feel most comfortable with. As an adult, it could be a friend, colleague or partner. If you suspect or know your child is being bullied, encourage them to talk to you or perhaps a teacher or another relative. If you don't get the response or the help you hoped for, choose someone else and carry on until you do. In addition to advice on dealing with bullying, there are numerous organisations that are set up to offer help, some with helplines or text services to contact in a crisis. If you ever feel in immediate, serious danger you should call 999 (UK), 911 (US) or 000 (Australia).

UK

Ditchthelabel.org is an international anti-bullying charity offering online help via digital mentors and a support forum. You can also call them on **01273 201129** between 9am to 5.30pm, Monday to Friday.

-

Actagainstbullying.org is a registered charity set up by the parent of a bullied child. It offers lots of advice for teenagers – you can also email them at: **info@actagainstbullying.org**

-

Antibullyingpro.com has an online support centre and offers a 24/7 crisis messenger service for young people in the UK – text **DA** to **85258.**

-

Childline.org.uk has some great practical advice, including how to deal with different forms of online bullying and an under 18s helpline: **0800 1111.**

-

Nationalbullyinghelpline.co.uk can be contacted on **0845 2255 787**, Monday-Friday, 9am to 5pm, and is aimed at both young people and their parents.

-

Giveusashout provides a crisis text support service for all ages – text **Shout** to **85258.**

USA

The National Suicide Prevention Lifeline provides 24/7 emotional support to people in suicidal crisis or emotional distress: **1-800-273-8255.**

-

Teen Line provides emotional support to young people: **teenlineonline.org/talk-now** **310-855-HOPE** or **800-TLC-TEEN.**

-

Covenant House NineLine deals with crisis intervention and angry feelings: **1-800-999-9999.**

-

National Hopeline connects callers to a 24-hour crisis center in their area: **1-800-784-2433.**

AUSTRALIA

headspace helps young people aged 12–25 years who are going through a tough time. Visit headspace.org.au or call **1800 650 890.**

-

Kids Helpline offers a 24/7 telephone and online counselling and support service for young people aged 5–25 years. Visit **kidshelpline.com.au** or call **1800 55 1800.**

-

Lifeline provides crisis support 24/7 for all ages. Call **13 11 14** or chat online every night at **lifeline.org.au.**

The emotional rollercoaster

Emotional problems are incredibly common in those with ADHD, from emotional dysregulation to meltdowns. Fortunately, there are ways you can help yourself

Words Alice Pattillo

Do you often feel like you are at the mercy of your emotions? Like you're always one accidental drink spillage away from a devastated sob or one 'constructive' criticism away from screaming the house down? You are not alone. More often than not, people with ADHD have trouble managing their emotions. While ADHDers no doubt experience the same emotions as everyone else, it is common for people with ADHD to experience emotions differently to neurotypicals, particularly in terms of their intensity and longevity.

One Cambridge study revealed that one in two children with ADHD experience emotional difficulties - namely explosive outbursts, depression and anxiety. What's more, many ADHDers have problems understanding their own emotions and recalling feelings. Children with ADHD often find it difficult to recognise less intense emotions as they are so used to emotions being stronger and all-encompassing. This behaviour can be traced to a defining characteristic of ADHD: emotional dysregulation.

Out of balance

Dysregulation in general is a hallmark of ADHD. It's dysregulation and not, as many believe, a deficit in attention that ADHDers struggle with; it's the inability to regulate their attention - leading to procrastination, distraction and hyperfocus. But it isn't just with attention that this dysregulation occurs, it's with everything - from hyperactivity, executive functioning, working memory and decision paralysis, to impulsivity and emotional responses. This lack of regulation is what gives ADHDers a seemingly all-or-nothing attitude. Someone with ADHD will give up on a project or issue due to suddenly feeling overwhelmed with stress or in reaction to feeling discouraged.

> "People with ADHD have trouble managing their emotions"

While everyone, including those with ADHD, becomes more adept at handling their emotions as they mature, many adults with ADHD still struggle with responding to emotional experiences.

The inability to control emotions can be one of the most challenging aspects of ADHD and leads to problems in all areas of life. In fact, emotional difficulties are likely to blame for the symptoms of depression and relationship problems commonly seen in people with ADHD. For example, inappropriate responses and 'overreactions' can cause social friction, rejection and troubles with friendships and romantic partnerships. ADHDers can find it difficult to be patient, prone to losing their temper, have outbursts or meltdowns and can be irrational and impulsive - following their heart and not their head.

Usually these emotional episodes are relatively short-lived, but unfortunately the relationship between emotional outbursts and ADHD isn't widely acknowledged and this can lead to further ostracisation from peers. We understand that meltdowns and sensory overload are key components of Autistic

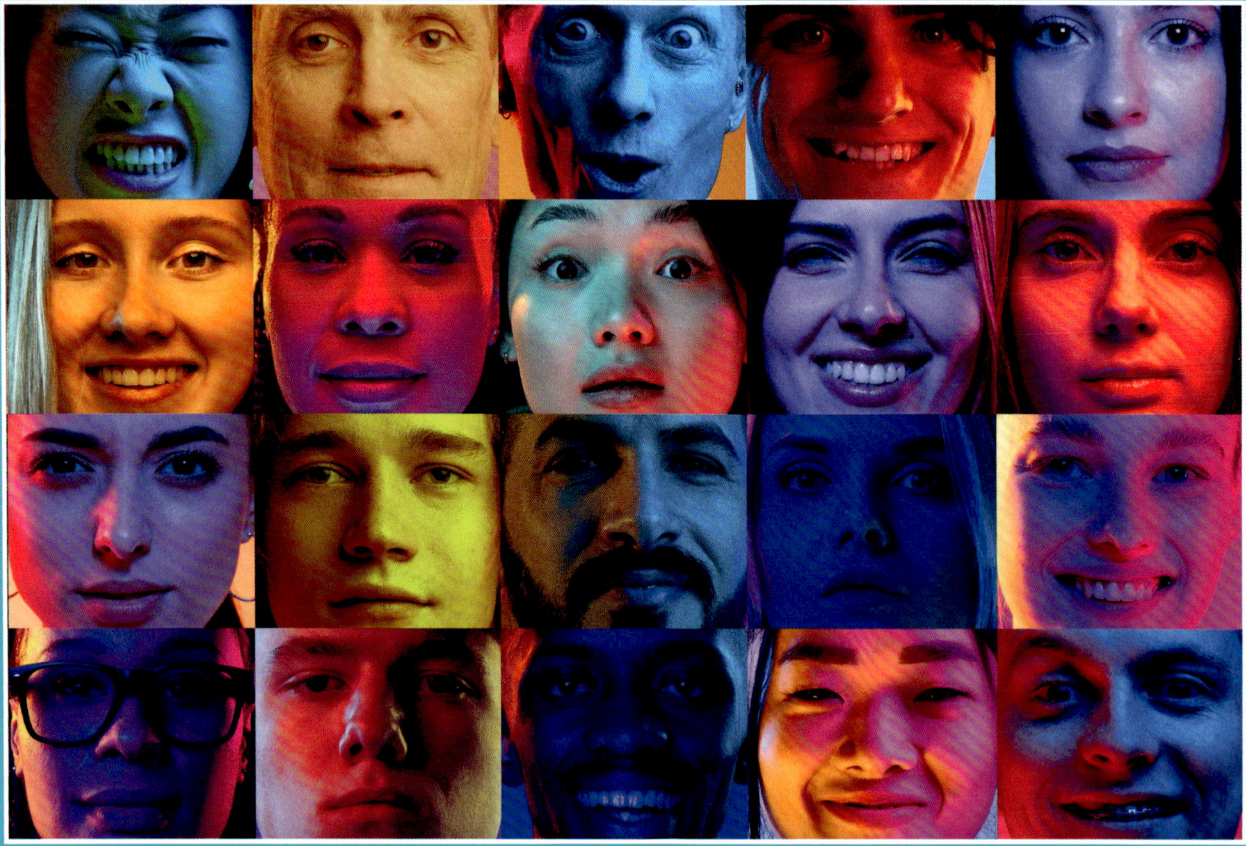

Spectrum Disorder, for example, but very few realise it is a common aspect of ADHD too.

> **"Intense emotional responses are often hyperaroused reactions"**

Extreme expressions

Those with ADHD often contend with numerous contradicting feelings all at once. Emotions may last a long time and trigger a negative spiral or happen in short, sharp bursts. Fluctuations are common, leading outsiders to see them as prone to mood swings - but these intense emotional responses are often hyperaroused reactions rather than true changes in mood. Those with ADHD are not inherently moody.

Hyperarousal causes an abnormal spike in responsiveness to various stimuli and those with it will often be diagnosed with anxiety and other mental health and mood disorders. However, moods have no clear starting point, no tangible cause and can last days or even longer. By contrast, emotions are reactive, high intensity, immediate and short-lived.

While ADHD is most commonly associated with physical hyperactivity, the majority of those with ADHD experience an internalised form of hyperactivity. Their brains are a constant storm of rattling thoughts, an internal shouting match that resembles the trading floor of the New York Stock Exchange back in the 1980s. It is impossible to switch off. More often than not, this mental cacophony of notions also manifests itself as emotional extremities, a form of emotional dysregulation known as hyperarousal. Hyperarousal is a state of heightened awareness and anxiety that is common in people with ADHD but also those who have experienced trauma. Among the neurodivergent, particularly those who went undiagnosed for a large portion of their lives, trauma is common - so it is more than likely that those with ADHD will experience emotional hyperarousal.

Barely holding it together

Other symptoms of hyperarousal include unconscious physical activity, such as fidgeting and restless legs syndrome, second screening while you watch TV or restlessness while attempting to do something mindless. Then there are breakdowns or meltdowns; chronic feelings of overwhelm; racing thoughts; overthinking; spiralling; and wallowing – being stuck on an idea or thought but not being able to move away from it no matter how hard you try to accept it.

People with hyperarousal are often criticised for being 'too much', 'too sensitive' or 'irrational'. They are told they are weird or impossible to deal with. They endure sleep problems and imposter syndrome. Personal and professional relationships often suffer from their knee-jerk emotional reactions that can cause them to say and do things they later regret. Hyperarousal also causes ADHDers to have a heightened sensitivity to any perceived criticism, teasing and rejection. All of this often leads to low self-esteem.

Passion paralysis

While ADHD can amplify emotions, it can be contradictory and also be responsible for freezing them out. It's common for ADHDers to have emotional shutdowns, where they are so overwhelmed by the intensity and number of emotions they are experiencing that their brains switch into survival mode and disassociate.

With the sheer volume of emotions that ADHD people experience, it's unsurprising that emotional burnout occurs, which essentially shuts down the brain. ADHDers avoid emotions as trauma has taught them that strong emotions lead to negative outcomes – so instead of the 'fight' response being activated, their brains learn to self-soothe by shutting down and freezing. In this state they may struggle to articulate any feelings they may have, feel numb, or struggle to speak and move entirely – and it can take a while to process emotions enough to formulate a reaction and show any of their usual intensity. This ability protects them from the extreme results of their meltdowns or explosive reactions and can mean ADHDers are remarkably resilient, despite seeming dramatic and fragile when in certain states. However, it also makes it hard for neurotypicals to tell whether or not they really care.

Conflicting compassion

For ADHDers, executive dysfunction paired with emotional dysregulation can make it difficult to interpret their own emotions and understand their true feelings. One moment a person could have a powerful, disproportionate reaction to a situation, and the next they could feel nothing for something that should evoke a profound emotional response. This can make it confusing for those around someone with ADHD. It can also make a person doubt their own emotions and feel like they lack the appropriate response, resulting in guilt and concerns that they are wrong, different and defective.

As well as managing behaviours, emotional dysregulation can have an effect on empathy. ADHDers may find it hard to recognise emotions in both themselves and others, and appear self-centered or remote thanks to poor attention span and impulse control. However, due to their emotional sensitivity, ADHDers actually have a deep capacity for empathy - the way in which they display it is just misunderstood. They have a unique ability to relate others' situations to their own, genuinely listening and putting themselves in their shoes, making ADHDers genuinely caring and amazing friends. Neurotypicals, however, might interpret an ADHDer relating

their experience to their own as self-absorbed, and the fact that they can recognise someone's pain but impulsively interrupt them to enthusiastically reassure them they get it, as making it all about them.

Someone with ADHD often feels too much, and has extreme and unfounded feelings of guilt, sentimentality, and rejection when they let others down. Many can understand others' feelings before they express them, and can foretell how someone might feel about a situation due to their restless mind

> **"ADHDers may find it hard to recognise emotions in themselves and others"**

whirring away and overthinking every possible outcome.

One aspect of empathy in which they most often struggle is having compassion for themselves. ADHDers internalise the criticisms they receive from their peers and authority figures and blame themselves for not being able to manage things that appear so easy for others. ADHDers strive for perfection and to do things independently, never feeling good enough and beating themselves up over their perceived failures.

Feeling the fall out

For an ADHDer, emotions are an orchestra hooked up to an amplifier with no volume dial - and when you power up, it's at stadium-level loudness. When you are dealing with an assault of high-level all-consuming emotion, it is almost impossible to self-regulate your behaviour. The immense level of noise buzzing around in your head means logical thoughts can't be heard and other senses are drowned out, and you fail to consider your actions and the consequences as you cannot access this part of your brain. ADHDers are unaware of the world outside their own deafening, emotionally strung-out brain as appearing to others as childish, inconsiderate and dramatic. Their meltdowns evoke harsh judgement and are akin to a child's tantrum - something people are expected to grow out of. This emotional dysregulation is linked to other ADHD symptoms, such as sensory overload, poor working memory and executive dysfunction. In fact, all ADHD symptoms have an impact on emotions in some way. There is also a knock-on effect between all of these symptoms - they can influence one another and cause deep levels of long-term emotional distress.

Other ADHD symptoms can trigger emotions too, creating a vicious cycle. Having too much external stimuli, such as being thrown into a noisy and crowded space and experiencing sensory overload, can easily trigger a meltdown, which can then manifest itself as snappy, nasty behaviours and a complete disregard for others in that moment.

ADHDers' tendency towards impulsivity also plays an unconscious role as it causes extreme emotional fluctuations, but their emotional dysregulation can also push them to act more impulsively and make rash decisions in order to get a quick fix, self-soothe and release endorphins in order to overcome the very real pain they are experiencing.

In moments of extreme emotional distress they can push people away and say things they don't mean. For a neurotypical, these sorts of episodes will be few and far between, but for someone dealing with ADHD, sensory

Rejection sensitive dysphoria (RSD)

A widely experienced symptom of ADHD that isn't really talked about is RSD - or rejection sensitive dysphoria - and it is heavily linked to how emotions are processed. The condition is an extreme version of what is known as rejection sensitivity and causes sufferers to experience a high level of emotional pain when rejection or criticism - real or perceived - is experienced. This emotional pain is extreme and overwhelming, a good way to describe it is grief - where an ADHDer has a profound feeling that they have lost love, approval or respect of a loved one. RSD is a form of emotional dysregulation, but not everyone with emotional dysregulation has RSD. It is thought it is more common in ADHD and autistic people not only because of their trouble processing information and regulating emotions, but also due to traumas and repeated social rejection - which itself, according to studies, triggers similar brain activity to pain.

Common RSD symptoms:

- Easily embarrassed and self-conscious
- Low self-esteem and lack of belief in yourself
- Problems managing emotions when faced with rejection, visibly seen in outbursts of extreme emotions such as rage or bursting into tears or sudden shifts into depression and periods of self-isolation
- Avoidance of starting tasks or beginning projects where there is a chance of failure
- Perfectionism
- Anxiety
- Self-sabotage
- People-pleasing

overload, emotional dysregulation, hyperarousal and rejection sensitive dysphoria, paired with the high-pressured, stressful, non-stop nature of our modern lifestyles, means it could be something that happens regularly.

And while someone might move on in a matter of minutes, the consequences to their lives and the effects their behaviours and words have on others can be significant, and saying 'sorry' might not be enough to fix it. Someone with ADHD is then left isolated, feeling embarrassed and humiliated, riddled with regret, self-blame and shame, which can spiral and ultimately lead to low self-esteem.

An ADHDer might feel like a burden to their loved ones and may also struggle to progress in life due to interpersonal relationships being tarnished or even destroyed due to their lack of ability to control behaviours triggered by emotional reactions.

Cry me a river

Both meltdowns and shutdowns are common in neurodivergents and are usually looked down upon by society. Meltdowns, where extreme emotions build up so much that they overwhelm the person and drive them to act out (often in the form of shouting, screaming, crying, laughing, throwing things, venting anger and energy, often all at once) resemble tantrums in children. But these tantrums continue into adulthood in ADHDers, leading to social isolation, embarrassment, guilt and shame.

Shutdowns, where someone is so overwhelmed by emotions they disassociate and become completely numb, can similarly isolate a person as they struggle to explain their feelings. It often makes them seem uncaring and unsympathetic.

But meltdowns and shutdowns are actually an important coping mechanism and way to regulate emotions. As babies we quickly learn these self-soothing methods, but as we age we learn that society deems a lot of them hallmarks of immaturity and prefers us to endure our feelings silently, chastising those who are fiery and spirited and marking them as irrational, and even crazy.

Crying in particular releases oxytocin and endorphins, activating the parasympathetic nervous system, which helps us to rest and recharge. These help to instantly relieve physical and emotional pain, resulting in a sense of calm and a return to baseline emotional arousal levels. So don't hold back your tears, it isn't shameful to cry.

© Getty Images / Adobe AI

> "Meltdowns and shutdowns are actually an important coping mechanism"

Navigating the storm

The Western world has a detached attitude towards an ADHDer's feelings, favouring quiet endurance over unbridled emotions, which can be particularly difficult for ADHDers. In a world where stoicism is celebrated it can be difficult to be somebody who feels so deeply. With such shame attached to some of their natural self-soothing methods, many ADHDers instead turn to unhealthy coping mechanisms, such as binge eating, gambling and overspending, alcohol and illicit substances, addictions and hyperfixations. Therefore, it is vital to learn healthy ways of channelling and filtering unruly emotions.

Breathing techniques, such as diaphragmatic breathing, can help to calm physical reactions by slowing the heart rate, while music can help to promote calm, as can getting outside for some fresh air. Meditation is another great way to help manage emotional dysregulation – in fact, it can help to rewire the brain and enhance the executive functions.

Another important way to help self-soothe is exercise. By physically exerting yourself you are channelling that emotional energy into physical energy and releasing it. On top of this, exercise releases endorphins, dopamine and serotonin, which all quickly elevate your mood. Exercise is an invaluable tool for ADHDers and you don't have to run a marathon – just 20 minutes of moderate movement a day and you will reap the benefits.

Working on your working memory may also help you to navigate your emotional extremities as ADHDers' working memory impairments have a significant effect on the way their brain processes emotions. Working memory requires the ability to tune out distractions and ignore irrelevant information, something they notoriously find almost impossible. With a poor working memory, an otherwise fleeting emotion can become too intense and overwhelm. Studies have shown that working memory training, specifically that which targets attention control, can help to regulate emotion.

Feeling inferior

Neurodiverse people may struggle with low self-esteem, inferiority complex and imposter syndrome. We look at why that is and how to build self-confidence

Words Julie Bassett

Sometimes being neurodiverse can have an impact on both self-esteem and self-worth. One small UK study* found that adults with autism, for example, have significantly lower levels of both life satisfaction and self-esteem; something that researchers have also found in other neurodiversities, like ADHD.

Neurodiversity and self-esteem

Self-esteem is a person's perspective of their own value and worth, based on their internal beliefs and opinions. We usually form these beliefs through our interactions with those around us, and often compare ourselves to our peers. This can be influenced by how much we feel we belong in our environments. When we feel included, supported, accepted and respected, this can help us to form positive beliefs about who we are, which in turn boosts self-esteem.

For those with ADHD or other neurodiversities, certain experiences and environments can make it hard to experience this sense of belonging. For example, schooling and education is often based around academic success, conforming to rules and passing exams. If we struggle in any of these areas, it can mark us out as 'different' from a young age - a feeling that will then follow us into later life and make us question our self-worth and value. However, if we're able to experience a more inclusive and expressive environment, where other strengths like creativity, lateral thinking and individuality are encouraged, we might feel more like we belong, bolstering our self-esteem.

Unfortunately, society is built to predominately cater for the

> **"Society caters for the experience of a neurotypical population"**

experience of a neurotypical population. When we don't frequently interact with others who see and experience the world the same way, it can feel isolating, lonely and 'othering'. There are also certain stereotypes and stigma attached to being neurodiverse, and while things are changing, and there is a growing wave of acceptance, knowledge and understanding, it can be hard to let go of negative beliefs.

Inferiority and imposter syndrome

Neurodiverse people can sometimes feel 'inferior' to others, based on a perception of what is considered 'normal'. This can be exacerbated when there is a co-existing learning or developmental disability. Constantly having to face obstacles and find ways to overcome them can be exhausting, leaving a person feeling helpless and misunderstood.

This is why many neurodiverse people try and put on a front to fit in, acting in a way that mirrors what others do, and trying to control reactions and emotions. Often these feelings of inferiority can stem from specific experiences, such as being treated differently at school or being branded as 'naughty' when reacting to an overstimulating environment.

Neurodiverse people may also suffer from imposter syndrome. This is when someone feels like they're not worthy of success, friendships or relationships, or that they've somehow 'tricked' or 'cheated' their way into these positions, rather than recognising the strengths that got them there. They then might live in fear that someone will 'find them out'.

This is linked to those feelings of inferiority and low self-esteem, making it harder to recognise any hard work and accomplishments, and to be proud of them. The problem is that throughout our lives, we might have been told over and over what we can't do, rather than focusing on what we can. This is something that sticks and makes any form of success seem impossible to achieve.

Building self-confidence

There are ways to develop more resilience, boost self-esteem and grow in confidence, but it takes time to change a negative or fixed mindset into a positive one that is capable of growth.

The first stage is in acceptance. It's perfectly normal to be overwhelmed, angry or upset by ADHD and the challenges it presents. It's okay to explore those negative feelings, but, ultimately, by accepting the way things are, it makes it easier to move on and thrive. This can take time, but having a good social support network can help with this.

In order to shift your mindset, it's important to think about strengths instead of weaknesses, the 'can do' instead of the 'cannot'. What are you

"It's important to think about your strengths instead of weaknesses"

good at? What skills do you have that you can use in different ways? How does your neurodiversity help you to think in a different way, to be more creative, to find alternative solutions? What are you interested in? Are there groups or online forums where you can discuss your hobbies and areas of focus? Do you have exceptional attention to detail? Are you always honest? These are all incredible traits and skills that have high value. Developing a mindset that is based on these strengths and skills can help you to build confidence and acceptance in the person you are.

Seeking ways to be independent as much as possible can also help with self-confidence. If there are areas that you struggle with, then finding solutions and workarounds can empower you and reduce feelings of helplessness. Also, learn to be confident in expressing what you need to help you feel comfortable in your environment, or have a trusted person advocate for you and your needs.

Finally, looking after your health and wellbeing can help your self-confidence, too. Things like regular exercise, a varied diet, plenty of water, fresh air and good sleep – all as far as possible depending on any challenges you face in any of these areas – can help to boost self-esteem and confidence.

Developing self-awareness

Self-awareness helps us to learn who we are as a person, accepting those things that challenge us and focusing on our strengths. It can be hard to go on this journey of self-reflection at first, but the more you do it, the easier it becomes.

It means getting to know yourself, your traits, your habits and your feelings. Finding your triggers and responses, your experiences and your opinions. Some people find it helpful to use a journal to write this down; other might prefer a more visual form of expression. It can be useful to talk to someone you trust to get started; ask them what they think your strengths and unique traits are. This could be a family member, friend or even a professional. They often see strengths in us that we don't see ourselves. It means being honest about weaknesses and challenges too.

Mindfulness can help, as this can be useful for staying in the present, grounded and aware. This could be a form of meditation, for example, though if you struggle with racing thoughts, it can be hard to switch off. But you can be mindfully active too – walking, for example, around a park and noticing the things around you, what you can see, smell, touch and feel. Mindfulness can be useful for managing stress, anxiety and overall wellbeing.

*Tsermentseli S. 'Self-esteem moderates the impact of perceived social support on the life satisfaction of adults with autism spectrum disorder'. *Autism Dev Lang Impair.* 2022 Dec

Executive dysfunction

We explore what executive function is and how it can be impacted in those with ADHD

Words Julie Bassett

Executive dysfunction refers to a deficit or underdevelopment of important executive function skills. This can lead to a myriad of issues that impact on our ability to complete daily tasks, even if they are seemingly simple.

Executive dysfunction (sometimes called executive function disorder) is not a health condition on its own. It's a symptom of multiple other health conditions and relates to a deficit of core executive function skills. Some of the conditions that executive dysfunction has been linked to includes brain injuries, alcohol or substance misuse/ addiction, multiple sclerosis, stroke and dementia. It's also associated with mental health conditions like depression, anxiety and OCD, as well as neurological conditions like ADHD and autism. People can have executive dysfunction without ADHD, but having ADHD can impact on executive function.

How much a person with ADHD struggles with executive dysfunction is very individual. For some, it can lead to minor issues around planning that can be overcome with support, for example; for others, it can cause severe problems that need a much more robust care plan in place.

To begin, we'll explain what executive function is and how it works, before tackling executive dysfunction and what treatments and support are available.

What is executive function?

Executive function is a term used to describe a set of mental processes that our brain performs to help us tackle everyday tasks. We don't notice these processes happening, as they are mostly automatic and run in the background to enable us to achieve certain things and complete tasks. We call upon our executive functions daily, helping us to manage all the things we need to do.

Our executive function skills enable us to do things like plan and prioritise, set and meet goals, stay focused on a task, follow instructions or directions, control our emotions, practise self-discipline and manage multiple tasks at the same time. There are various analogies used to describe the role of executive function skills; sometimes it's referred to as the manager or administrator of the brain, and it's even been called the 'air traffic control centre' of the brain. These kinds of references can be useful in explaining just how complicated executive function is and how important it is.

We're not born with executive function skills already in place, though the potential to develop them is there. We build them through life experiences and practice. This starts from a very young age – babies begin to learn how to focus and pay attention to the people around them, and playing games such as peekaboo can help them to develop working memory and understand object permanence.

Executive function skills tend to develop most quickly between ages three and five. They continue to develop through childhood, during adolescence and late teens, and into adulthood. Executive function skills typically peak in your late-20s to early-30s, and they can decline again as we age. Women may find they experience changes with their executive function when going through menopause due to the fluctuations in hormone levels.

"Our executive function skills enable us to do things like plan and prioritise"

The main areas of executive function

Executive function can be broken down in different ways to help explain the many aspects of our brain that it helps to control.

For a start it helps to control our working memory, which is the memory we use to retain information in the short term, as well as action tasks. This includes things like remembering directions or following instructions, staying focused when reading and retaining what has just been read, and keeping up with a conversation. Essentially it enables us to process the information that we need to know in the moment,

while carrying on with whatever it is we're doing.

Then there is cognitive flexibility, which controls your brain's ability to be adaptable and change depending on the environment or external triggers. This means being able to switch between different tasks, or different parts of a task, and is important for solving problems and creative thinking. We use cognitive flexibility every day without even realising. Things like driving rely a lot on our ability to respond quickly to an ever-changing situation, and it helps us to cope with unexpected or unplanned occurrences.

Next is inhibitory control, which helps us to retain self-control, avoid impulsive behaviours and prioritise what needs to be done and when. It helps us respond to feelings and urges, prevents automatic responses, and enables us to apply reason to a situation before acting.

These three core executive functions have many sub-categories assigned to them, which all combine to build up a robust set of executive function skills (see the boxout, 'Examples of executive function'). These skills help us to pay attention, organise ourselves, plan and prioritise, complete tasks, regulate emotions and monitor our actions. Broadly, all of our executive function skills either fall into thinking skills or doing skills. Thinking skills relate to our cognition and understanding of different situations and tasks, whereas the doing skills relate to our behaviour in various situations and environments.

We usually take our executive function skills for granted; mostly they happen automatically in the background and enable us to complete daily tasks. It can be hard, therefore, to understand why we might struggle with something in our life that others seem to find easy. Executive function skills underpin so many different tasks and areas, it's no wonder that when there is a problem with executive function, it can lead to struggles and problems in lots of ways.

Examples of executive function

Executive function skills help us to do many daily tasks that we often take for granted. Here are some examples of what we use executive function for.

Quick tips for coping with executive dysfunction

Allow for time-blindness

If you're always underestimating how long something takes, make it a rule to allow extra time even if you think you don't need it. That way you don't have to rush, and if you finish early, you can do something you enjoy.

Don't overplan

You may be prone to planning more than you have capacity for, and this can cause frustration when it's impossible to follow through. Set limits on how many 'big' tasks you can assign to any one day.

Use reminders and alarms

Set reminders and alarms for everything, no matter how small. Factor in plenty of time before the task needs to be done to enable you to prepare.

Take notes

When you're in a meeting or talking to someone, write down notes or take voice notes. As soon as you think of something, write it down too, no matter what it is - something you need to get from the shop, a birthday, a bill to pay, etc.

Create a routine

Assign weekly tasks to a specific day and make sure that daily tasks are somewhere you will see them when you get up in the morning. Some people like lists, whereas others prefer more visual cues.

Signs of executive dysfunction

Executive dysfunction is when we have a disruption in usual executive function. It is described as a 'behavioural symptom' and affects our ability to manage our thoughts, emotions and behaviours. This will impact on an individual in different ways, depending on which core executive functions are impacted. Many of the symptoms we commonly associate with ADHD are also symptoms of executive dysfunction, so the two do overlap.

Those with ADHD may not develop executive function skills in the same way or at the same time as their peers, which can mean that they struggle with situations that require a certain degree of executive function. Those with ADHD might know what they need to do and how to do it, but struggle with putting it in to action or getting started. It's normal to have strengths and weaknesses when it comes to executive function with both a neurotypical or neurodiverse brain; however those with ADHD might find themselves facing more challenges with more types of executive function and with greater severity.

Executive dysfunction can lead to problems with time management, for example. This can include things like not being able to accurately judge how long things will take, which can mean putting off getting started (procrastinating) because it feels like there's more time than there is, or needing to rush at the last minute to meet a deadline. This is sometimes called 'time blindness', which is the inability to gauge how much time has passed or how much time is needed.

> **"A person can know they need to start or finish a task, but lack the capacity"**

A person with executive dysfunction may also struggle with controlling their impulses. This can lead to things like interrupting people in conversation rather than waiting for their turn to talk, buying things impulsively, saying things that are inappropriate or engaging in risky behaviour.

Another area that can be impacted is organisation. This can make it hard to stick to a routine day to day, as well as keep track of appointments or meetings. This might mean that a person struggles to remember to eat regularly, for example, to get enough sleep or do enough exercise. This isn't down to a lack of intention; most people are aware of what they need to do, but still can't do it. Even when systems are put in place, it can be hard to maintain them.

This links in to starting and completing tasks. It can be hard to start tasks in the first place, which can lead to procrastination or avoidance. Once started, a person might be easily distracted and leave tasks unfinished or lose focus, meaning that things are left half done or not done at all. Again, the intention is there, and a person can know that they need to start or finish a task, but lack the capacity to take action.

Executive dysfunction can affect working memory, meaning that a person may find they are frequently losing items or documents they need, which can be incredibly frustrating.

Impact on health and wellbeing

If you recognise these symptoms, then you may have some degree of executive dysfunction. Everyone

has issues in some of these areas at some point, as we can struggle with executive function when we're overtired, going through a lot of stress or feeling rundown or ill. However, for someone with ADHD, these kinds of problems are ongoing and numerous, which can make doing normal everyday tasks much harder.

Executive dysfunction and ADHD can then impact on wider health and wellbeing. It can create a lot of stress for a start, especially when it comes to meeting deadlines, missing important meetings or finding it hard to stick to a routine. This can impact on a person's ability to look after their home effectively or succeed at work, which can create stressful environments.

It can also influence personal relationships. Friends might feel neglected due to a person not replying to messages or not feeling listened to. Family members can find it frustrating when someone is constantly late or disorganised. This can create anxiety in the person with executive dysfunction, as well as worry about letting others down.

This can all have a knock-on effect on self-esteem, as a person with ADHD might wonder why they can't do these 'simple' tasks and they may not feel like they're 'good enough' or even that they're 'stupid' for not being able to do the things that come so easily to others. Over time, this can raise the risk of mental health conditions like depression.

Executive dysfunction can also lead to a decline in physical health. A person may find it hard to get enough good-quality sleep, or to stick to a physical exercise routine. They may also struggle with preparing meals and eating regularly, or remembering to take medication or drink enough water.

> **"It can take some trial and error to find the strategies that work for you"**

Treatment and tools for executive dysfunction

Living with executive dysfunction can be hard. It's exhausting and all-consuming, taking more energy than it should to be able to do normal everyday activities. However, there is help available. It's not a 'one size fits all' set of solutions, however, so it can take some trial and error to find the right strategies that work for you. The aim of support tools is to make it easier to navigate daily life.

In terms of treatment, it's important to take any prescribed ADHD medication, as this can help with some of the underlying causes and make it a little easier to be in the right mindset to tackle executive dysfunction. Cognitive behavioural therapy (CBT) can also be suitable for some people with ADHD and executive dysfunction, as this can teach important skills and help you understand and come to terms with your abilities. Lifestyle can help too, as things like regular exercise, a balanced diet and enough sleep can all boost executive function, as well as alleviating some of the symptoms of ADHD.

Many people with executive dysfunction rely on the use of planners and task managers to help them stay on top of what they need to do. It can seem very overwhelming putting new systems in place, and they won't always work. Start small and try implementing one thing at a time. This might be a daily to-do list of what you need to get done, including everything from small tasks like putting a load of washing on and taking it out again, to larger things like work deadlines. It can be helpful to include a daily walk or exercise, or even mealtimes, to ensure these are also done. Large calendars with appointments on in a place you look at often can be helpful, and task management apps can automate a lot of your diary requirements, helping you to plan your day. There are apps aimed at those with ADHD that are tailored to support you.

Having a solid routine can limit the need to make too many decisions each day. It can be difficult to stick to a new routine, but the aim is to try to as much as possible and each day, hopefully it will get a little easier. Break down daily tasks into smaller steps, as this can make them easier to achieve. So, rather than saying 'get ready', you can break it down into what that means step by step. You may also want to introduce reward systems for motivation; if you complete all your tasks or stay focused on a larger task for a set amount of time, you might then reward yourself with time to read or look at your phone, for example - just don't forget to set an alarm for when your downtime ends, as it's easy to lose track of time when you're doing something you enjoy.

The aim is to adapt your environment to work with your executive function challenges, rather than fighting to try and get your brain to work in a more typical way. This can be a less stressful way of living and can ease some of the worry and anxiety that surrounds executive dysfunction.

Spot executive dysfunction in children

Children can't always explain or understand what they're struggling with. If you have a child with ADHD, or suspect they have ADHD, you may spot that they have symptoms of executive dysfunction. Remember that executive function skills are still developing in childhood and adolescence, but you may notice that they are learning these skills at a different time to their peers.

Examples that may become clear are things like having trouble planning ahead or often losing things - this can be more obvious in the later school years when they may find it hard to keep track of homework assignments or follow a timetable. They may struggle with time, often losing track of time or being late, and they may also find it hard to stay focused and pay attention, which is something that can affect school progress. Children can lack self-control and act impulsively, and may find it hard to understand things from other perspectives. You can work with your children to help develop executive function skills, as well as put into place different strategies to help them stay organised. The main thing is to ensure that they feel supported and cared for, which can help with their self-esteem and self-confidence.

Feeling overwhelmed

We explore why those with ADHD and other neurodiversities experience overwhelm and how to handle it

Words Julie Bassett

Overwhelm describes any situation where something becomes just too much for the available resources to handle. In terms of the brain, overwhelm is a response to feeling overcome with thoughts, emotions, physical feelings and/or situations that are more than you're able to process and cope with. Everyone, whether neurodiverse or not, can become overwhelmed, particularly in times of high stress, however for those with a neurodiversity, feeling overwhelmed can happen more often.

This is because neurodiverse people have to not only cope with the usual causes of stress and strain, but are also living in a world that is ultimately designed around a more neurotypical experience. This creates an environment that is inherently a source of stress and triggers, although individual causes of overwhelm will vary.

> "Some neurodiverse people find it harder to handle social engagements"

Why do we experience overwhelm?

There are many reasons why those with a neurodiversity will experience overwhelm. For some people, particularly those with ADHD or autism, senses can be heightened, meaning that a person is sensitive to light, sound, texture or smells. In a situation where there is, for example, a lot of loud, overlapping noises, it's not uncommon for someone who has heightened sensory processing to become easily overwhelmed and overstimulated.

Another trigger can be certain social situations. Some neurodiverse people find it harder to handle social engagements, especially if they find it difficult to follow the thread of a conversation, don't always pick up on social expectations or cues, find it hard to know when to talk or respond, or can't easily identify another person's emotions or feelings in conversation. This can mean that it's more difficult to stay engaged and can be an exhausting experience, especially if concentrating on masking, which can lead to being more overwhelmed.

Change, especially unexpected or sudden change, can lead to becoming overwhelmed too. Some neurodiverse people use routine and structure to help navigate day-to-day life, and disruptions to this can be difficult to cope with. The threshold for change varies hugely. While for one neurodiverse person it can be a big change like moving house that triggers overwhelm, for another it can be a bus not turning up or a particular item being out of stock in a shop that has the same reaction.

Decision-making can also be a trigger for overwhelm, especially if someone feels that they are being asked a lot of questions or having to navigate a lot of situations at once.

For those who struggle in a specific area, such as in the case of dyslexia, it can be hard to avoid the things they struggle with, which can also build up into feeling overwhelmed.

Other common reasons for overwhelm include clutter, disorganisation, trying to focus on a lot of tasks, deadlines and planning.

Neurodiversity is complex and it's important to note that while the triggers may change from person to person, the feeling of being overwhelmed is something that can impact physically, mentally and emotionally regardless of the cause. Overwhelm can also build up if not identified and supported properly, meaning that our ability to cope with further triggers is compromised. Overwhelm can snowball and lower our tolerance to particular situations, which can lead to anxiety, poor mental health and lower self-esteem.

Effects of overwhelm

When we do get overwhelmed, this can manifest in a lot of different ways. Some people will feel the overwhelm in a very physical way, which can be in a racing heart, a tight chest or difficulty breathing, headaches, visual disturbances, feeling hot or cold, and dizziness. Emotionally, it's not uncommon to feel very anxious or stressed, frustrated, irritable or angry, sad or teary.

It can also lead to some people feeling restless, unable to sit still or needing to pace; others may have to use physical ticks or stimming behaviours as a way to try and block out the overwhelming sensations. Repetition in movement or thought, being unable to sleep, finding it hard to focus and concentrate, and exhibiting impulsive behaviour can all be caused by being overwhelmed.

If overwhelm isn't supported or dealt with, and therefore carries on over a long period of time, chronic overwhelm can ultimately lead to burnout (see the boxout, right).

> **"When we do get overwhelmed, this can manifest in a lot of different ways"**

Coping with overwhelm

It can be incredibly hard to cope with overwhelm, and strategies to do so very much depend on the age, capacity and ability of the neurodiverse person, as well as the specific difficulties and the severity of those difficulties that they may face.

If the overwhelm is sudden and immediate, then the most important

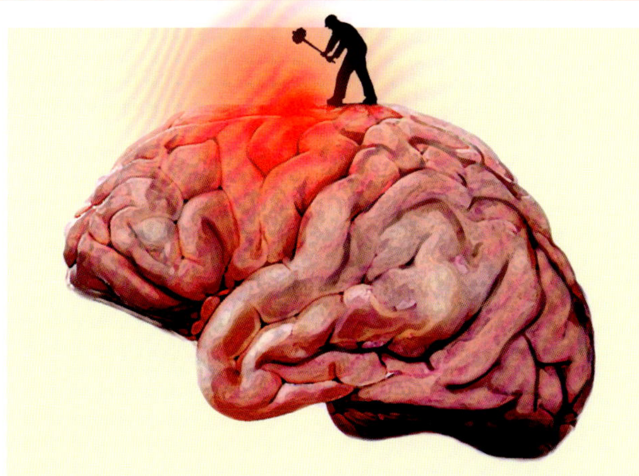

When overwhelm leads to burnout

Feeling overwhelmed a lot of the time and for a long time can lead to burnout. Burnout is caused by long-term stress triggering the brain and body to essentially 'shut down'. Burnout can cause symptoms like chronic exhaustion, anxiety, irritability, physical issues, an inability to focus, insomnia and feeling unable to cope.

Neurodiverse people may be more likely to experience burnout due to the extra challenges they face in having to adapt to an environment that's not optimised for them. This can be especially true if someone spends a lot of time masking in order to fit in at work or in social situations, or adapting and engaging in situations in which they don't feel comfortable.

Some studies show that neurodivergent people may experience burnout differently to neurotypical people, and that symptoms can vary depending on the type of neurodiversity – this can include things like a loss of skills, increase in sensory sensitivity and needing more support than usual in daily activities.

It's important to seek help in the case of burnout, as it doesn't often get better on its own without intervention, and recovery can take weeks or months.

Tips for prioritising

If you're looking at your to-do list and feeling overwhelmed, here are some tips for prioritising your tasks:

Not everything is urgent

When you write a list, it gives everything equal urgency. One method to prioritise is the Eisenhower Matrix, which breaks tasks down by urgency and importance, separating tasks into Do Now (things that are important and urgent), Decide Later (things that are important but not urgent), Delegate (things that are urgent but not important) and Delete (things that are not urgent or important).

Do quick tasks

Handle any tasks that will take less than 5 minutes right away. This is great for those little tasks like washing up, taking laundry out of the machine, opening mail, etc, that can easily turn into bigger tasks if not done. Some people respond to gamifying these little tasks with reward systems or timers.

Daily tasks

When a task has to be completed every day, build a daily routine that ticks them off. If you struggle to cook, for example, then meal planning, batch cooking and prepping ingredients in advance can help. Every morning, assign 5 minutes to make your bed, and every evening use 10 minutes to tidy a room. These routines will build and become habit, while chipping away at overwhelm.

> "Self-soothing in the moment can stop the feelings from building up"

thing is to try and remove the trigger and find a safe space. If it's a noisy environment, for example, is there a quieter area nearby to take a few breaths and calm down? Some people find sensory objects useful to have in a pocket, which can be used when overwhelmed as a focus or distraction. Self-soothing in the moment can stop the feelings from building up, which can include strategies like visualisation, getting fresh air, practising a breathing technique or repeating certain phrases or affirmations.

The more you understand your neurodiversity and what can trigger you into feeling overwhelmed, the more you can plan and prepare. The first step is in learning your own personal triggers and recognising the signs of overwhelm before they build up. This gives you time to extract yourself from a specific situation, or to notice when life's daily tasks are starting to build up to an unmanageable level so that you know you need to step back.

Some people might find it useful to make a list of what is making them feel overwhelmed if it's task based; although for others, a list can be a source of overwhelm if it's hard to then delegate or time manage that list - proving that there is no one solution to managing overwhelm that suits everyone.

Long term, prevention is always better than cure. Make sure that you're taking time for yourself. Some neurodiverse people find that journalling, lists, breathing activities, exercise or meditation can help prevent overwhelm from building up. It's also good to spend some time exploring thoughts and feelings to try and understand where they're coming from, and learning to reframe negative thoughts - some people may need external help with doing this and education around different coping tools and techniques.

The key thing is not to ignore these feelings of overwhelm. It's a valid emotional response and being mindful to it can help with understanding, seeking support and coping better with day-to-day life.

A matter of interest

ADHD and its impact on attention and motivation is often misunderstood but the interest-based nervous system offers a fresh, alternative framework for comprehending this unique neurological profile

Words Emma Green

The term attention deficit hyperactivity disorder (ADHD) may be widely recognised these days but it is often criticised for not reflecting an accurate portrayal of the lived experiences of those diagnosed with the condition. Only in recent decades has the Diagnostic and Statistical Manual of Mental Disorders (DSM) formally recognised ADHD symptoms in adults and yet the three core features it outlines - inattention, impulsivity and hyperactivity - do very little to capture the breadth or nature of the disorder.

The reference to 'attention deficit' suggests that those with the condition lack focus when in reality, this couldn't be further from the truth. "I often say to people that you have an abundance of attention, not a deficit," says Dr Sarah Carty, founder of ADHDdoc, a GP-led service that diagnoses and treats adults with suspected ADHD. "The issue is that you can't regulate it."

A growing body of research is now calling for a more nuanced and informed explanation of the unique patterns of attention and motivation in individuals with ADHD. An example of this is the concept of the interest-based nervous system, which is finally shifting the dialogue surrounding ADHD from one of deficit to one of difference.

Interest-based vs importance-based nervous systems

The human nervous system is a marvel of complexity, guiding everything from reflexive actions to intricate cognitive processes. While research has previously focused on its biological, chemical and anatomical foundations, more is now being learnt about its role as a driver of neural function and behaviour.

Dr William Dodson, a psychiatrist specialising in ADHD, coined the term 'interest-based nervous system' to describe the distinct way that people with ADHD are motivated and how their attention is directed. According to Dr Dodson, those with an interest-based nervous system are governed by tasks that are engrossing, novel, and enjoyable. However, they don't respond well to the incentives that usually drive neurotypical people, which are things like rewards, fear of consequences or societal expectations.

"It is thought that if you are neurotypical, which is about 90% of the world's population, you have an importance-based nervous system," says Dr Carty. "So, when you do something, it's because it is deemed important by you, your family or the world around you, such as having a good job or buying a house. If you have ADHD though, you have a different type of nervous system and can find it hard to be motivated by things considered important to neurotypicals."

ADHD brains often prioritise immediate rewards over delayed outcomes, a trait that aligns with the interest-based nervous system's preference for doing tasks that feel engaging in the present moment.

> **"If you have ADHD, you have a different type of nervous system"**

Long-term goals can feel abstract and this disconnection makes it harder for those with ADHD to sustain consistent effort on a project or activity over time.

The interest-based nervous system acts as a filter, directing attention toward stimuli, tasks or ideas that are inherently interesting or emotionally meaningful. When a task aligns with someone's passions, the ADHD brain is more likely to react positively and override the typical distractibility of the condition, leading to greater focus and creativity when approaching said task. However, someone with ADHD may struggle to initiate or complete tasks they perceive as uninteresting compared with neurotypicals who find it easier to engage with both fun and monotonous tasks. This lack of response from the nervous system to low-reward stimuli can lead to frustration, chronic procrastination and even avoidance of certain tasks.

"It's the struggle to do the tedious, the mundane and the boring things," says Dr Carty. "I often find patients have done huge amounts of research on ADHD before I see them because it's very interesting to them. Yet that same person could not sit down and go through an article that their boss has asked them to read, even though it's important."

Motivators of the interest-based nervous system

Dr Dodson identified four key motivators that stem from the interest-based nervous system and rouse the ADHD brain. He proposed that a task will be completed if it meets at least one of the following criteria within his ICNU framework: that is, if the task is Interesting, a Challenge, Novel or Urgent.

The interest-based nervous system is highly sensitive to intrinsic interest and is naturally drawn to stimuli that spark its curiosity. It could be argued that most people would prefer to pursue activities that excite them, but for individuals with ADHD, these tasks often take priority, even when neglecting other tasks could result in severe repercussions. ADHDers have a tendency to rotate rapidly through different interests, developing a hyperfixation for something before shortly abandoning it for something else - hence why someone with ADHD is sometimes cited as having a 'graveyard of unfinished hobbies'. For those with both autism and ADHD (AuDHD) however, their passions can be far more enduring and are usually referred to as 'special interests', due to the niche and extensive knowledge they often possess.

ADHD brains thrive on stimulation, and a challenge or competition can make a task far more attractive to them. A task that involves some difficulty can prompt the interest-based nervous system to go into problem-solving mode, channelling both intense focus and determination to overcome the high-stakes situation because the payoff - an immense

"Novelty is a powerful motivator for the interest-based nervous system"

feeling of satisfaction and pride - is worth the amount of exertion involved. The trick, though, is striking the right balance. Too much difficulty or challenge can be overwhelming to the ADHD brain and can result in procrastination or complete avoidance altogether. Furthermore, if the payoff is too far off into the future or will take a long time to achieve, motivation can soon wane.

Novelty is another powerful motivator for the interest-based nervous system, especially if the task feels new or different from what has been done before. This isn't just limited to starting new projects - shiny new tools, routines or hacks can revitalise old and mundane habits by injecting some much-needed freshness and inspiration into them, whether that's buying a new planner to get organised, signing up for the gym or trying out the latest cleaning fad. The problem is that novelty is short-lived and while it can spark an initial surge in momentum, maintaining this engagement over time can be difficult once the activity becomes

ADHD and hyperfocus: a double-edged sword

ADHD is often associated with difficulties in sustaining concentration, yet one paradoxical aspect of the condition is its ability to hyperfocus - a state of intense, almost obsessive absorption on a specific task or activity for extended periods. This phenomenon is often described as the polar opposite of the distractibility commonly linked with ADHD. During hyperfocus, attention is laser-sharp, distractions fade away, and time seems to fly by.

"Being able to hyperfocus is an amazing gift," says Dr Carty. "The issue is that it is very hit and miss as to when you can do it."

Hyperfocusing has been likened to the concept of 'flow', a term coined by psychologist Mihaly Csikszentmihalyi, which refers to the mental state achieved when a person is fully immersed in an activity and experiences a sense of energised focus and seemingly effortless concentration. It is also used to describe someone who is working at peak performance. Flow, however, is a much more controlled and balanced state and is highly conducive to positive wellbeing and productivity, while hyperfocusing can be both a strength (when it's harnessed properly) and a challenge (when it leads to the neglect of other tasks or responsibilities).

repetitive or routine. The interest-based nervous system is always on the lookout for new stimuli and so novelty alone cannot be relied upon to maintain long-term and consistent input with a project or a habit.

Meeting deadlines is a common motivator for most neurotypical people but for someone with an interest-based nervous system, action is only triggered in cases of extreme urgency, high-pressure situations or when facing immediate consequences. The ADHD brain responds strongly to the adrenaline rush created by time pressure, which can provide a much-needed burst of energy in completing a task. This is one of the reasons why those with ADHD tend to procrastinate or leave things to the last minute – while others would crumble under the stress, the ADHDer flourishes, often zoning in and disregarding all other tasks and distractions. Time-sensitive opportunities provide swift rewards or at least a sense of relief, once the clock has been beaten and the task accomplished. However, relying on extreme urgency and crisis as a motivator can be detrimental to the ADHDer's physical and mental health. Being exposed to chronic stress can lead to inconsistent performance, anxiety and burnout as well as adverse effects on the cardiovascular, immune, digestive and endocrine systems.

> "The ADHD brain responds to the adrenaline rush created by time pressure"

The neurological reasons for the interest-based nervous system

There is increasing evidence, thanks to advances in neuroscience, that shows that ADHD brains deviate from their neurotypical counterparts in their structure, connectivity, and neurochemical balances. These physical variances provide clarification as to why those with ADHD respond to stimuli and regulate attention differently to others - and not because of some kind of character deficiency.

One major difference is the overall structure and volume of the ADHD brain. MRI scans have shown that ADHD brains tend to have slightly smaller overall volume, especially in regions like the prefrontal cortex, basal ganglia, and cerebellum. The development of the prefrontal cortex, which is responsible for executive functions such as planning, making decisions, and impulse control, is often delayed in those with ADHD. This, coupled with its smaller volume and impaired communication between the prefrontal cortex and other brain regions, can lead to difficulties when it comes to regulating attention, emotions, and behaviour.

"The prefrontal cortex is the secretary of the brain," says Dr Carty. "It's the organiser, the planner, the part of the brain that prioritises, starts and finishes tasks. That's the part of the brain that is underperforming and has always been underperforming."

Another key difference is the discrepancies in the availability of certain neurotransmitters that fuel the brain's reward system. Dopamine plays a crucial role in motivation and reward processing and when dopamine is released in response to certain stimuli, that stimuli is then associated with pleasure. ADHD brains often have lower baseline levels of dopamine, making it harder for them to feel motivated by tasks that aren't immediately interesting or rewarding. Some studies have suggested that this might be due to fewer dopamine receptors in certain brain regions, such as the prefrontal cortex, while other research has proposed that the increased activity of dopamine transporters in ADHD brains leads to a faster reuptake between neurons, reducing its ability to stay in the system for long enough. Another affected neurotransmitter is norepinephrine, which works together with dopamine to regulate attention and arousal. Dopamine dysregulation can disrupt norepinephrine signalling, compounding difficulties in focus and task engagement.

This shortfall in dopamine can explain why those with ADHD tend to have an interest-based nervous system. Novel and interesting stimuli activate dopaminergic pathways, which reinforce behaviours that lead to pleasurable or fulfilling outcomes. It is understandable then why those with ADHD would prefer to chase dopamine-inducing incentives

ADHD and procrastination

The flip side of hyperfocus is procrastination, where low-interest or challenging tasks that feel insurmountable are delayed or avoided. Although procrastination is a common human affliction, it can be particularly debilitating for those with ADHD. Issues regarding executive dysfunction, emotional dysregulation, impulsiveness and time blindness that are associated with the condition can exacerbate putting off tasks.

"People describe procrastination as having a block between what they know they need to do and actually doing it," says Dr Carty. "The whole condition of ADHD is not a knowledge-based problem but a performance issue. ADHDers self-medicate by procrastinating because when a task becomes urgent, they get a dopamine surge which gets them moving. However, it can also cause a rise in the stress hormone cortisol and living under that degree of stress all the time is really not good for mental or physical health."

Someone with ADHD might engage in productive procrastination, where they complete other useful errands instead of tackling the overwhelming task. This might be organising a workspace, doing laundry or cleaning the house instead of working on a more cognitively challenging project or studying for an exam. Low-stakes tasks like these can offer a quick burst of motivation but they can also give a false sense of progress if used to evade stressful yet usually more valuable tasks.

Using interest-based motivators to your advantage

Learning to embrace your interest-based nervous system rather than trying to fight against it or fix it can be transformational for those with ADHD. Adapting tasks so that they incorporate intrinsic motivators rather than relying on traditional external incentives, such as rewards or deadlines, can enhance productivity and help ADHDers to fulfil their true potential.

To add interest to an activity, you could pair a tedious task like cleaning with a favourite playlist or audiobook, use fun tools such as colourful stationery or personalise a project by using visual or multimedia elements.

To add an element of competition, you could try 'gamifying' routine tasks by setting personal challenges, assigning points to tasks or logging progress through visual aids like charts and graphs.

To add novelty, try rotating different work environments, study methods or hacks to keep a habit interesting. Try swapping continuously between low-interest and high-interest tasks for variety.

To add a sense of urgency, set a timer, find an accountability partner, or 'body double' with someone else while completing a challenging task.

whenever the opportunity arises to compensate for its scarcity, as opposed to activities or tasks that fail to deliver the same degree of this feel-good chemical.

Benefits and problems of the interest-based nervous system

The distinct neurological wiring of the ADHD brain can prove to be both a remarkable asset and a significant liability. Its ability to hyperfocus on passion projects can foster great creativity and innovation as well as ground-breaking ideas. Possessing a brain that is built 'different', coupled with interest-driven attention, enables someone with ADHD to engage in outside-the-box thinking, often developing unconventional solutions that others might not have thought of. This may explain why those with ADHD tend to gravitate towards self-employment, as this grants them the freedom and flexibility to dive into their chosen area of interest and to choose how they approach their work.

Another major virtue of the interest-based nervous system is its ability to flourish in chaos. The ADHD brain excels in fast-paced or unpredictable settings, often being able to think quickly and juggle multiple tasks at once. "ADHDers are brilliant in a crisis," says Dr Carty. "They're totally unflappable. Jobs in the emergency services are where people with ADHD can really excel."

The most significant drawback of the interest-based nervous system is that it doesn't always serve the individual's broader needs. Interest-based attention can make it challenging to prioritise tasks effectively. Choosing immediate gratification and interesting activities over long-term goals and necessary but boring tasks, means that day-to-day responsibilities can fall through the cracks. An interest-based nervous system can also encourage ADHD individuals to act impulsively without considering long-term ramifications. This can manifest in abandoning projects or commitments once the novelty has worn off or chasing unhealthy dopamine fixes, such as overspending or living off a diet of junk food.

The interest-based nervous system can also create fluctuations in energy and productivity, which can result in problems in maintaining consistent performance. When the system is thriving, it can produce exceptional results but if it is thwarted in any way, it can result in decreased output.

Living in an importance-based world with ADHD

For those living with an interest-based nervous system, there can be a considerable mismatch between their reliance on intrinsic interest to sustain attention and effort and the societal systems they must navigate. Traditional school and work environments tend to emphasise structure, routine, and motivators such as grades or deadlines, which can fail to engage the ADHD brain. This misalignment can often result in shame, underachievement and

burnout from trying to fit into a society that is designed around importance-based expectations.

An overhaul is needed, on both an individual and systemic level, in how society views both conventional notions of productivity and the contributions of its neurodivergent members. "I think at the end of the day it comes down to understanding that some people process the world differently," says Dr Carty. "It's like a different culture. Judging others is much easier than someone working on becoming a better communicator, for example. It's not that the neurodivergent person is lazy; they just need a little bit more checking in with and more instruction on what is expected of them."

> **"The ADHD brain excels in fast-paced or unpredictable settings"**

Rather than perceiving ADHD as a flaw, the interest-based nervous system theory provides an empowering narrative for understanding how the ADHD brain works and how it can thrive under the right conditions. Finding ways to incorporate interest-driven approaches, such as allowing personalisation of tasks, could revolutionise education and workplaces for the better and allow those with ADHD to share their gifts, for everyone's benefit.

Improve your memory and concentration

Tips and tricks to boost your working memory and focus

Words Julie Bassett

Having ADHD can come with certain challenges around memory and concentration. Due to the differences in the way a neurodivergent brain processes and retains information, those with ADHD might have issues with both short- and long-term memory, as well as concentrating and staying focused. This can then impact on productivity, completing tasks and following instructions.

However, it's important to remember that processing things in a different way isn't a bad thing; it just means that you might need to adopt different strategies than a neurotypical person. Memory, like any other function, can be strengthened and improved, and there are numerous techniques that can boost concentration – you just need to find what works for you.

How your memory works

The way the brain processes information and retains it for future recall is complex. First, we have to take in and understand new information, then we have to store it, and finally we have to be able to retrieve it later on. It takes thousands and thousands of minute connections in the brain to complete this process, but it doesn't take much to disrupt it. Everyone has moments of forgetfulness, but those with a neurodivergent brain may struggle with memory more often than a neurotypical person would.

ADHD is linked to having a poor working memory. This is the type of memory function that enables us to take in information and action it to complete a task – things like remembering where your keys are, creating a mental shopping list or holding on to a person's name during a conversation. Our working memory can hold multiple pieces of information at the same time, and some people are able to hold more information than others.

Having a weaker working memory can affect day-to-day life in lots of different ways, such as losing items frequently, forgetting passages you've just read, missing deadlines or forgetting to finish things you've already started. It can come across to others as not paying attention, being disorganised or not listening. And it can become very overwhelming trying to remember everything, not drop any balls and to stay focused.

Recognising that your working memory needs a little help means you can put strategies in place to compensate, rather than beating yourself up over your perceived limitations. It can take a bit of planning and organisation to get yourself set up with the right tools, but it can make a huge difference to your daily activities.

> "Recognising your working memory needs help means you can put strategies in place to compensate"

Improve your memory

Routine and consistency are your friends. The more you do something, the easier it becomes. Essentially, you're turning daily tasks into habits that you perform automatically. You might create a routine for first thing in the morning where you do everything in the same order and go through it step by step so that one action triggers the next. Or you might create a routine that you follow every time you go in your house that includes putting your keys in the same place immediately before you can get distracted.

Repetition can help store details in your memory – which is why routines work well. When someone gives you an instruction, try repeating it back to them by saying something like, 'just to confirm, you want me to...', helping to create a stronger link in your working memory.

A smartphone is helpful for things like setting alarms and reminders, using the notes function to keep lists, and a calendar that you input events or meetings in to as soon as you know about them, with an associated reminder a week, day and hour before. Manual lists are also useful, as are apps that help you to track habits. You can also leave sticky notes in useful places, so they trigger your memory when you see them. Some people work better with visuals rather than words, so you might find it easier to associate mental pictures with certain things you need to remember, like people's names or shopping lists.

Try and avoid multitasking wherever possible. This can make you feel like you're being less productive, but actually you'll get more done if you focus on one thing at a time. Trying to do lots of things at once makes it harder for the working memory to retain all the different bits of information.

Boost your concentration

Many of the techniques for memory will also help with your concentration. By making tasks less overwhelming and breaking them down into smaller parts, it's easier to focus on them one bit at a time. This means that for every big task, break it down into smaller steps and just tackle the first step before moving on. It can help to set a deadline for each step too, as it's easier to focus when there's an end goal.

One of the problems with staying focused and concentrating on the task in hand is that we suddenly think of other tasks or errands, or get distracted by something more interesting, and we can lose time on those thoughts rather than staying on task. Many people with ADHD find

it helpful to have a notepad close to hand so that when these thoughts pop up, they can write them down and come back to them later. Part of the reason we find ourselves going down rabbit holes or suddenly researching something that we've just thought of is triggered by a fear that we'll forget about it, so having a place to write down all these thoughts and tasks can relieve some of that worry.

It's also easier to concentrate when you remove distractions - this might mean using headphones, turning off the radio or television, working on an uncluttered desk and turning off notifications on your phone. Plan in regular breaks too, which can help you to stay focused, knowing you have a chance to take a break at a set time.

By leveraging these tools, you can make real improvements to your memory and concentration. However, it's also important to accept the differences in your memory function and focus, and stop putting pressure on yourself. Work with your brain, not against it, and you'll find ways to make daily life easier to handle.

"Many techniques for memory will also help with your concentration"

Brain-training activities

Working memory can be improved by training your brain and stretching its capabilities. This can include doing things like puzzles or memory games. There are lots of apps for smartphones that offer brain-training activities based around memory, repetition and cognition. These can be helpful if you prefer to do things in a digital environment, and if you do them every day, you can see an improvement in your working memory.

Try and complete offline puzzles too, such as doing crossword puzzles, where you need to recall facts and information to solve the clues, sudoku and similar number-based puzzles, or board games. Jigsaw puzzles are good too, as you need to use your working memory to help you bring the picture together, and things like LEGO can help you to practise following instructions. You can also challenge yourself by remembering a list of words or reciting facts. You can ask a friend or family member to help as well, by setting up visual memory games or asking them to quiz you on a set of information.

Whatever you choose should be fun, so that you're more likely to stay interested in it and keep practising.

How to avoid seeing red

Discover how to master your anger response, learn to use it to your advantage, and diffuse difficult situations

Words Julie Bassett

Anger, like joy or sadness, is a normal emotion, one that we have all experienced and will continue to experience. It's a natural response to a situation in which we're frustrated, irritated or provoked.

In situations that trigger us, the body gets ready for 'fight or flight', with anger readying us for the fight option. It's normal, even good for us, to feel anger sometimes, especially when it's justified - anger enables us to express a negative reaction to a situation, rather than bottling it up inside, and it makes us want to seek out solutions to problems. But for the neurodiverse, anger can become all-consuming, an instinctual reaction to simple frustrations or difficulties that can negatively impact your day-to-day life.

While it might be one of the 'basic' human emotions, it's also incredibly complicated, and we all have our own individual thresholds of what causes us to feel anger.

What is anger?

Anger is an emotional response, a reaction to a situation where you feel challenged, criticised or your boundaries overstepped. It is an intense emotion that can leave you feeling stressed, frustrated, annoyed and irritated, but there are also different levels of anger. It can range from minor annoyance, through to controlled rage and even irrational overreaction.

The triggers for our anger are unique; what fills one person with seething rage might simply be a minor inconvenience for another. It can be useful, especially for children, helping us to learn right from wrong, and showing us where our morals and values lie.

When something bothers us and we feel anger, this can manifest both physically and mentally. You might feel tense and tight, get a headache or jaw ache, feel hot and sweaty, notice your heart pounding, or experience racing thoughts. You may find it hard to focus or concentrate, and be less in control of your emotions. Inside your body, your brain is sensing danger and will release adrenaline (to prepare you for a stressful or dangerous situation), noradrenaline (involved in cognitive function and stress reactions) and cortisol

> “We all have our own individual thresholds of what causes us to feel anger”

(typically in response to high anxiety and stress).

Some people internalise this anger, but dwell on it in their thoughts; others react more verbally in the moment, shouting for example. Others have more extreme reactions, tending towards aggression, causing damage or seeking revenge.

There are different types of anger. There is anger towards wider, global issues, for example the kind of anger we might feel towards political bodies, our treatment of the environment, wars and disasters. In these cases, we might feel helpless and sad that we can't help, or we might feel motivated by our anger to react, through donating funds, attending protests and using our vote.

Then there is justified anger in situations we face in our personal lives, such as when a partner lets us down, we're stolen from, or someone accuses us of something.

Finally, there is anger that comes from annoyance or frustration, when we usually know we're overreacting, such as when driving, walking behind someone who is slower than us, waiting in queues, or being put on hold on the phone.

Anger is usually caused when something happens that is at odds with our expectations. For example, we expect a loved one not to cheat on us and feel betrayed if they do. If we expect to be able to park outside our house, but someone is already in our space, we might feel a flash of anger and irritation.

So, feeling anger is often outside our control, as our body is flooded with hormones in response to a trigger, but what we can influence is how we react to it. This is where our brain kicks in, specifically our prefrontal cortex, responsible for decision making, which helps us to put that anger into context and react in an appropriate way.

How we respond to anger

Not all of us respond to anger in the same way. Children find it much harder to react in perspective and are more likely to shout, cry, break something or hurt themselves. They haven't yet developed the control and understanding that's needed to process the intensity of anger. Their world is much smaller, so when something doesn't meet their expectations – even something as simple as expecting the blue cup with their dinner – their body triggers an anger response and they don't know what to do with it. It's up to the adults in their lives – parents, teachers and older siblings, for example – to help them learn to recognise the signs of anger and

"It's quite normal to feel anger from time to time, but frequent or excessive anger can have dire results"

explain different techniques to handle those feelings.

But even as adults, we don't all have the same ability to regulate and control our anger response. This can stem from childhood, if we've never been shown how to handle anger or we've been taught to repress it.

Some personality traits are also linked to anger. Someone with underlying mental health conditions, such as anxiety, OCD or depression, may feel more anger as situations are less likely to meet their expectations and they may fixate on those things in their lives that cause sadness and frustration. Some people may find it hard to be agreeable, wanting things to happen their way and being unable to be flexible emotionally to see things from another perspective. There can be a sense of entitlement, or a belief that their own views are in some way superior and should be adhered to. Some people might fixate on things that are out of their control, blame others for their own situations, struggle to regulate their emotions, or have a low tolerance for feeling uncomfortable.

None of these is necessarily a negative personality trait, and feeling anger is not a weakness. If someone has perfectionist tendencies, for example, they might be high achieving, get great results and do well at work, but also find it harder to accept 'less than' and feel angry when things are not perfect.

We can also find it harder to control our anger when we're under a lot of stress, experiencing grief or loss, or going through major life changes. This can affect our tolerance, and anger can flare in situations when it wouldn't usually – the proverbial straw that broke the camel's back, as it were.

Anger can also feel good sometimes, reassuring us that we know where our morals stand, that we know what's right and wrong, and it can teach us how we feel about situations.

It's often considered that men get angrier than women, but research* shows that the frequency and intensity of anger is not impacted by our gender. However, the way in which we express our anger can be different.

While this is somewhat generalising, men might be more likely to express anger in an outward way, shouting, pushing, through aggression or hostility; whereas women might simmer, turn their anger inwards, engage in passive behaviour like sulking, and fixate on situations and conversations in their mind. In part, this is societal - aggression and masculinity have often gone hand in hand, while women who show anger can be called irrational or overly emotional.

There are problems with both types of response, and there are issues with these ingrained stereotypes. It can lead to women feeling unable to express their anger, meaning that the things that trigger them continue to happen, leading to wider issues, such as stress, anxiety and depression; and men can feel unable to express their anger through non-aggressive means, finding it hard to talk about what they're feeling and ask for help.

How to manage and cope with anger

Learning to cope with anger is a key life skill. It's quite normal to feel anger from time to time, but frequent or excessive anger can have huge consequences. Because being angry raises stress hormones, blood pressure and heart rate, long-term anger can increase your risk of health conditions like coronary heart disease, type 2 diabetes and stroke.

Also, if your anger levels are elevated, you might find that you overreact more easily in different situations, or you might engage in compulsive and unhealthy behaviours, such as smoking, drinking more than usual or lashing out. Feeling angry can also make us more impulsive and prone to making irrational or sudden decisions.

There are two key areas to focus on when it comes to anger management: how you react in the moment and how you can improve your wellbeing so that you're less likely to anger in the first place. When you're in a situation that creates anger, you need to learn how to control your response (see the box to the right for some quick ways to diffuse) in a rational way. This doesn't mean suppressing the fact that you're angry - it means taking time to think about what you want to say or do. Rather than shouting and clenching, breathe and say something like, 'This situation is making me feel angry because...'. It's important to acknowledge anger as an emotion and try to drill into what

"As hard as it is to cope with our own anger response, it can be even harder to cope with another person's"

it's trying to tell you about the way you feel.

If anger is taking over in your life, then you need to look at your lifestyle and how you can make improvements so that you're less likely to boil over. Practising relaxation techniques on a regular basis can help to keep stress at bay, doing things like meditation, breathing exercises, going for a massage treatment or yoga. Make sure that you're sleeping enough, as when you're tired you are far less likely to be able to cope with a situation that induces anger. Exercise is also important. It can help to maintain lower stress levels, but it's also a good outlet for excess anger, channelling it into something physical and helping to calm your mind. Having a chance to talk to someone you trust regularly can also help with feelings of anger building up and getting out of control.

As hard as it is to learn to manage and cope with our own anger response, it can be even harder to cope with another person's, especially when it's someone we're close to. It's natural to take it personally and this can make us feel angry ourselves, or less worthy. But remember that anger is a response and it doesn't always reflect a person's true feelings; they may be reacting impulsively and not be thinking clearly. Try to give them space and respect their boundaries; let them work through why they're angry in their own time. If you push for a response or an apology, this can sometimes fuel the anger and lead to an argument on both sides. If you can, stay calm, but if you can't, it may be best to extract yourself from the situation while you both take a little time to think. Set your own boundaries too, as actions caused by anger can be damaging, and you need to be clear about what behaviour is unacceptable to you for the sake of your own wellbeing.

We're not seeking to eliminate anger; anger is a core emotion that can drive us and steer us. The key is in mastering it, learning to recognise it and control it, before it controls you.

5 ways to diffuse anger fast

Walk away

If you're in a situation that's making you angry, walk away. Go outside, make a hot drink, sit down quietly - whatever helps you to calm down and think more rationally.

Breathe

Breathe in and out, deeply and slowly, which can help you regain control over your emotions and steady your mind. You may like to count your breath in and out as well.

Ground yourself

Bring yourself into the present moment by focusing on something you can touch, something you can see, something you can hear and something you can smell.

Be honest

Recognise that you're feeling angry and express that. If someone else is involved in the situation, tell them that you're feeling angry and that you need to regroup before continuing.

Visualise

Close your eyes and imagine a place that makes you feel calm, whether that's by the sea, in the forest or up a mountain.

*Dittmann, M. 'Anger across the gender divide'. Monitor on Psychology (2003)

The 'F' word

When friends seem to be few and far between, ADHD could be the underlying culprit playing havoc with your friendships and social life

Words Emma Green

We all know that friendships play a pivotal role in boosting the quality of our lives - whether that's through providing support, companionship or a sense of belonging. What is less known, though, is the direct hand that our friendships have in our life's potential quantity. Researchers at Brigham Young University correlated data from 148 longitudinal studies and found that those with strong social ties have a 50% greater chance of life longevity than those with weaker connections.

As important as it is to have a strong support system around us, for many with ADHD, their attempts at trying to build and maintain friendships over the years are too often a solemn tale riddled with mishaps, disappointments and disillusionment. With an estimated 3-4% of the adult population having ADHD, how can this demographic learn to navigate a domain that so often eludes them?

ADHD and social development

As children, we learn social skills, such as listening, making conversation and reading non-verbal cues through observational learning, usually by watching and copying others. Children with ADHD, however, often struggle to master these essential skills due to the challenges that arise from the core symptoms of their condition - impulsivity, inattention and hyperactivity. Impulsivity can manifest in behaviours such as blurting things out without thinking, dominating conversations or constantly interrupting others. Inattention can present as being easily distracted, showing disinterest or struggling to stay on topic during a conversation. Hyperactivity, meanwhile, can appear as being overly talkative, too loud or coming across as boisterous or aggressive.

While ADHD affects everyone differently and can depend on the type that someone has, certain deficits in executive functioning, such as difficulties in regulating emotions or reading social cues, can make it even harder for children with ADHD to interpret and manoeuvre social dynamics effectively. Children with ADHD often struggle to relate to their peers of the same age, preferring to socialise and play with younger children. This may be due to the later maturation of certain brain structures in those with ADHD such as the cortex, which is responsible for attention, planning and complex thought processes.

Because of this delay in development, children with ADHD are quite often misunderstood or worse, rejected by their peers. Research has indicated that not only are they more likely to have fewer friends and less satisfying friendships than neurotypical children, but they are

> **"ADHD children have fewer opportunities to practise and hone their social skills"**

four times more likely to be victims of bullying too.

As positive relations with peers play an important role in a child's social development, this can create a vicious cycle of ADHD children having fewer opportunities to practise and hone their social skills, further delaying social functioning. Their repeatedly failed attempts at socialising can become associated with feelings of exclusion, humiliation and shame, potentially leading them to simply want to avoid it altogether.

How ADHD can affect friendships

Social relations become even more complex as children enter their teens and then adulthood. Forming and maintaining friendships as an adult can be a challenge for most people, without the structure of school or extra-curricular activities to facilitate this, but for those with ADHD, it can prove even harder. The skills required to maintain friendships, such as setting up plans and following through with them or remembering to check in regularly with friends, need effective executive functioning, something that those with ADHD are not typically great at. Furthermore, behaviours caused by executive dysfunction can be interpreted by others as flakiness, rudeness or simply a lack of care.

One example of this is forgetfulness. Memory issues are common with ADHD, usually resulting in missed birthdays and anniversaries, unanswered texts or forgetting key information such as the names of a friend's kids. This absent-mindedness can give the impression of being unreliable or uncaring, which can strain friendships over time. "I recently forgot my best friend's birthday," says Lucinda, who was diagnosed with ADHD inattentive type in her thirties. "It wasn't even that I forgot - I knew it was her birthday and that I needed to send her a card and a present but I kept putting it off. I felt so guilty that I then isolated myself and couldn't message her."

This forgetfulness might be a result of something called object permanence. People with ADHD are prone to forgetting about tasks, objects and even people that aren't immediately visible or engaging, a sort of 'out of sight, out of mind' phenomenon. For instance, they might forget to respond to messages or fail to reach out to someone for months at a time simply because the visual cue isn't a constant in their

immediate environment. As our lives become more digitalised and there is less physical overlap with friends, it's easy to see how friendships can often slip through the net.

Another related difficulty is inconsistency. ADHD can cause fluctuations in mood and energy, leading to periods where someone might socially withdraw and be unreachable for a while and yet at other times, they might be eager to socialise and engage with others. Inconsistency can also present as a pattern of last-minute cancellations, as those with ADHD can struggle to stick to plans that were made weeks or months in advance. This can be confusing for those on the receiving end and this unpredictability can make it hard to sustain friendships. Even when they do manage to carry out their social commitments, difficulties with focus, attention and listening may hinder their friendships further. Oversharing, zoning out halfway through a conversation or constantly interrupting others can make it hard for friends to feel valued or heard.

Emotional dysregulation is also a common, but often overlooked, symptom of ADHD, although it is not a diagnostic criterion for the condition itself. Emotional dysregulation refers to difficulties in managing and regulating emotional responses, which often results in intense or disproportionate reactions to situations. It can present as heightened sensitivity, ruminating on a negative comment or perceived

Improving social skills 101

In most cases, people with ADHD know what it is they should do to improve their social skills but struggle to implement them – another classic hallmark of the condition. Fortunately, social skills can be developed and strengthened through targeted practise and making small deliberate tweaks over time can make a big difference.

The first step is to cultivate self-awareness around how your ADHD behaviours affect your social interactions. You could do this by consciously monitoring yourself, recording conversations or roping in someone to gently point out any social cues you may have missed or any social faux pas you may have made without realising. Observing how others interact or watching their body language can help to give further insight.

Another necessary step is finding a trusted friend or therapist to act as a 'friendship coach' to practise your social skills with. Role-playing different social situations together or rehearsing 'social scripts' in a safe space can give you the necessary confidence to navigate everyday social interactions. Pick a skill you would like to work on, such as active listening or not interrupting others, and then enlist your designated coach to give you honest feedback on your performance.

Making and keeping friends

Avoid avoidance

It may be easier said than done but you need to put yourself out there on a regular basis. Socialising and the curation of friendships are lifelong habits that we must implement consistently. By setting yourself targets such as talking to a set number of people each time you're in a social situation, you can find a new-found purpose to keep trying.

Consider disclosing your condition

Being upfront about your condition can help to prevent any misinterpretations of your behaviour and encourage others to be supportive, instead of feeling hurt or ignored by you.

Find people with shared interests

Finding groups or clubs based on something you're passionate about - whether it's a sport, hobby, or volunteer activity - can make socialising feel natural. When you're engaged in something you love, it's easier to feel more comfortable starting conversations and finding others who share your enthusiasm.

Block out time for socialising

Designating specific times, like Sunday evenings, for communication, can prevent relationships from fading. Set aside a few minutes each week to send texts or check in on friends. Even short messages like "Hey, just thinking of you!" can go a long way in maintaining connections.

slight for days on end, lashing out at others or rapid shifts in moods. This volatility can be misinterpreted as being overly dramatic or moody and friends may distance themselves as they're uncertain about how to handle the friendship.

Some people with ADHD may turn to masking as a coping mechanism for dealing with social difficulties. By suppressing or altering their ADHD behaviours, they can attempt to fit in socially and avoid negative judgments. "It can be quite difficult," says Lucinda. "You try to put on this best version of yourself which is exhausting, so then you withdraw because you don't have the energy to be that person anymore."

How comorbidities further impact friendship

ADHD is associated with several mental health problems that can make social interactions even more difficult. One example of this is rejection sensitive dysphoria (RSD), a condition where individuals experience intense emotional responses to perceived rejection or criticism. Often affiliated with ADHD but not exclusive to it, RSD amplifies feelings of shame, disappointment, and insecurity in social interactions and can be an additional obstacle for those with ADHD in forming and maintaining friendships.

Kaylee, who was also diagnosed with ADHD in her thirties, knows this feeling only too well. "It's that dread of what other people think of you," she says. "You constantly think that people don't like you. Everything that you say or do, you think people will be talking and laughing about you behind your back."

If left unchecked, RSD can develop into social anxiety, which is a disorder characterised by an intense fear of social situations where someone may be judged,

> "Some people may turn to masking as a coping mechanism for dealing with social difficulties"

criticised, or embarrassed. It's not hard to see why ADHD and social anxiety might go hand-in-hand – having to constantly worry about making social gaffes would be enough to make anybody want to avoid socialising with others. "It's almost as if I don't want to bother making friends because there's this expectation that it isn't going to work out – because most of the time, it hasn't," explains Lucinda. In some cases, those with ADHD may stick with or settle for friends who treat them badly because they figure it is better than having no friends at all.

Other conditions which are common with ADHD are low self-esteem and depression. They can further inhibit motivation to socialise with others or encourage withdrawal altogether. "I think with ADHD symptoms, there's a lot of shame and guilt attached to them," says Lucinda. "There's so much talk about how humans are social beings so it's almost like a fundamental failing not to be able to socialise properly."

Benefits of ADHD friendship

Despite the challenges, there is so much that those with ADHD can contribute to their friendships. Many often bring a vibrant energy, unique perspectives and positive traits such as spontaneity, creativity and enthusiasm to their interactions with others. "People with ADHD are usually interesting people as they will go down rabbit holes when they hyperfocus," says Lucinda. "So they're good to have on a pub quiz team as they know so much random crap. They can also be quite fun to have around because they're constantly seeking that dopamine hit."

Those with ADHD are also often described as empathetic and accepting of others, as they know how it feels to be 'different' and misunderstood. "Those I know with ADHD, myself included, are very loyal," says Kaylee. "I might not always text you back but I will always be there for my friends."

The problem is because so little is known in the public consciousness about how ADHD behaviours affect friendships and socialising, those with ADHD don't always get the chance to share their unique strengths with others. "I have no animosity towards friends I've lost because of my poor friendship skills," says Lucinda. "If someone doesn't reply to texts or doesn't check in regularly, most people would assume that person doesn't like them or care about them. But if there was more awareness, people would know that ADHD behaviours aren't a reflection of how much they value you as a person – it's just a reflection of their condition."

Do narcissists target the neurodiverse?

Those with ADHD or other neurodiversities face a heightened risk of falling into abusive and trauma-bonded relationships, leading to a cycle of unhealthy partnerships. But it's not your fault – here's why...

Words Alice Pattillo

Navigating romantic relationships can be tough for anyone, but it's especially challenging for neurodivergent people, who are disproportionately affected by abuse, particularly from intimate partners. Studies reveal that women with ADHD are almost five times more likely to face physical abuse in a romantic partnership, while autistic individuals are three times more likely to experience bullying, physical, or sexual abuse. Disturbingly, almost nine out of ten autistic women have experienced sexual violence. So, why are neurodivergent individuals more vulnerable to domestic abuse, and crucially, what can be done to avoid these toxic relationships?

Opposites attract?

Research suggests that neurodivergent people might attract those with narcissistic or sociopathic traits, possibly because some neurodiverse traits mirror the behaviours of these toxic personalities. For instance, while autistic and ADHD individuals may appear self-focused due to compensating for their communication and sensory-processing difficulties, narcissists and sociopaths exhibit similar behaviours out of a belief in their own superiority. The overlap makes it easy for abusers to manipulate neurodivergent partners, projecting their own faults onto them and convincing others the neurodivergent partner is the problem. While narcissists and sociopaths lack empathy, autistic and ADHD people often have higher levels of it. This is appealing for a toxic personality, as they can exploit this sensitivity and tendency to forgive and see the best in people.

It's not me, it's you

Many neurodiverse individuals struggle with social interactions, leading to a lifetime of negative feedback that fosters low self-esteem. By age 12, neurodivergent children hear 20,000 more negative comments than their neurotypical peers, contributing to feelings of shame, guilt, and poor self-worth. This vulnerability makes them

“Many neurodiverse individuals struggle with social interactions”

prime targets for toxic partners who exploit their need for approval and acceptance. Years of bullying, communication difficulties, and social isolation exacerbate this risk, as abusers can more easily manipulate someone who already feels misunderstood and alone. Many neurodivergents are honest and blunt about their perceived failings too, which will boost a narcissist's need to feel superior.

Love is blind

Neurodivergent people often miss early signs of toxic behaviour due to their tolerance for others and struggles with interpreting social cues. Autistic individuals may take deceitful partners at face value, while those with ADHD may rush into relationships without recognising red flags. This tendency is particularly dangerous, as many neurodivergent people also struggle to communicate their own boundaries effectively and can therefore elevate their risk of being taken advantage of.

Feeling more deeply

Those with ADHD in particular often struggle with emotional hyperarousal, which causes thoughts, reactions and feelings to be more intense. Criticisms have more of a long-term effect on those with emotional hyperarousal - but so do feelings of love and pleasure. This makes it easier for people to love bomb them as they will associate them with the intense happiness, but also means any criticisms will be taken very personally and profoundly affect their self-esteem. It also elevates the risk of suffering from post-traumatic stress disorder and other disorders that can arise out of trauma, such as dissociative disorders, depression, anxiety disorders, borderline personality disorder, obsessive-compulsive or paranoid personality disorders.

You drive me crazy

Gaslighting, a common tactic of abusers, can have a profound impact on neurodivergent individuals who may already doubt their own memories and perceptions. ADHD affects working memory, causing minor details to be forgotten, while autistic individuals and those with dyslexia may also struggle with processing and recalling information. This makes it easier for abusers to distort reality, convincing their partners that they are the ones at fault.

Consistent gaslighting can lead neurodivergent individuals to hyperfixate on the idea that they are the problem, exacerbating their existing emotional dysregulation, eventually leading to meltdowns. These forced meltdowns give the abusers a chance to paint their partners as 'crazy' or aggressive. This manipulation not only damages the victim's self-perception but also enables the abuser to justify further punishment and control. Another worrying consequence is that studies show if police are called during an autistic meltdown, law enforcement often perceives the neurodivergent victim as the aggressor, leading to further victimisation.

You are my world!

Love bombing - a tactic where an abuser overwhelms their partner with excessive affection to gain control - is particularly effective on neurodivergent individuals, who may misinterpret this behaviour as genuine. Neurodivergent people may also engage in love bombing, though usually without malicious intent. Hyperfocus and intense interests are common traits in people with ADHD, and this can be misinterpreted as love bombing by their partners. Because of this, they may not recognise the abuser's behaviour as manipulative, making it easier for them to fall into

the trap. On top of this, love bombing can be intoxicating, as ADHDers often crave approval after a lifetime of criticism. However, love bombing can lead to trauma bonding, where the victim becomes addicted to the abuser's approval, despite the subsequent cycles of abuse. It can also result in isolation, as the victim becomes increasingly dependent on the abuser, neglecting other relationships and responsibilities.

Please don't leave

Rejection Sensitive Dysphoria (RSD), common in those with ADHD, makes the threat of rejection or abandonment especially painful. Abusers exploit this by threatening to leave, triggering intense reactions and further entrenching their control. Research indicates that social rejection activates brain regions associated with physical pain, making it especially hard for neurodivergent individuals to distinguish between emotional and physical threats, which can exacerbate emotional dysregulation.

Love conquers all

While neurodivergence can make someone more vulnerable to toxic relationships, it doesn't mean that you are doomed to be a victim.

Awareness of your own behaviour, as well as that of others, is crucial. Setting boundaries, documenting events, and building a support network can help protect against and break the cycle of abuse. Even then, abusers are skilled manipulators who exploit vulnerabilities.

Abuse is never your fault, and if you suspect you're in an unhealthy relationship, find help - in the UK visit **relate.org.uk**, try **talkspace.com** in the US, or **relationships.org.au** in Australia. Love should be honest, understanding, and supportive - never settle for less. Trust your instincts; if something feels off, it probably is.

Tolerating trauma

Post-traumatic stress disorder (PTSD) develops after experiencing a traumatic event, such as war or sexual violence, and is classified as an acquired neurodiversity. While around 40% of those with PTSD recover within a year of treatment, Complex PTSD (C-PTSD) results from prolonged trauma and often leads to additional conditions like anxiety, depression and substance abuse. Symptoms include nightmares, flashbacks, hyperarousal, and emotional numbing, with C-PTSD adding feelings of shame, guilt and relationship difficulties.

PTSD and C-PTSD are more prevalent among women and neurodiverse individuals. A 2021 survey found that 44% of autistic adults met the criteria for PTSD, while people with ADHD are four times more likely to develop PTSD than neurotypicals. Many C-PTSD symptoms overlap with ADHD, and those with ADHD and emotional hyperarousal often experience trauma more intensely, increasing the likelihood of PTSD after events that might not affect neurotypicals as much. Additionally, past trauma, whether diagnosed or not, heightens the risk of entering abusive, trauma-bonded relationships.

ADHD in the workplace

How the benefits and challenges of ADHD can lead to a fulfilling work life

Words Julia Mitchell

While the workplace can sometimes be challenging for people with ADHD, finding the right role and receiving the correct support can allow them to thrive. As with all individuals, living with ADHD can bring a variety of strengths that makes them invaluable members of their team, despite the difficulties that they may face.

If you or someone you know is living with ADHD, it's worth taking a moment to explore the many benefits that ADHD can bring to the workplace, which are extensive, and will vary from person to person. An increased likelihood for impulsivity can mean that individuals are quick to start on projects, and the ability to hyperfocus can be harnessed when the work aligns with their interests and strengths. Everyone is different, though, so it should also be remembered that the opposite can also be true - some people with ADHD may struggle with procrastination and beginning tasks, while others find it difficult to finish projects. Relationships with colleagues can also suffer if the team misinterprets their behaviour, perhaps assuming that

frequent lateness means that they don't care about being on time, or that difficulty meeting deadlines means that they don't care about their work. This is rarely true, but it's common for people with ADHD to worry about how they are perceived by others.

Some employees with ADHD may have a talent for problem solving and an increased ability to 'think outside the box'. It's also common for people with ADHD to show high levels of creativity, and research actually shows that people with ADHD tend to be more creative than those who do not. One interesting study found that, within a group of college students, those with ADHD had a preference for coming up with new ways to solve problems,

"Employees with ADHD are good at thinking up new ideas"

while those without preferred to use existing methods. When applied to the workplace, this could mean that employees with ADHD are strong innovators who are good at thinking up new ideas and ways of working.

Often the key to thriving at work with ADHD is to find a position that fits with a person's skills and interests. Although a repetitive administrative job may not seem appealing, other professions like teaching, journalism, healthcare and catering provide work environments that are more dynamic. People with ADHD are often able to stay calm in crisis situations, and their ability to keep their emotions under control while managing difficult and high pressure situations can make them ideal candidates for jobs in the emergency services.

"Specific workplace coaching is also available for people who have ADHD"

So, what should someone with ADHD look for in a job? As well as finding work that fits with their skills and interests, people with ADHD may find it helpful to work in a role that provides a structured day, with plenty of stimulation and opportunity for movement. It could also be useful to be able to access regular and fairly immediate feedback, in a way that doesn't leave them feeling too constricted and micromanaged. For jobs that don't offer these things, it's often possible to request adaptations that will make the workplace more accessible, and in many countries providing reasonable adjustments is a legal right.

The list of potential adjustments that can be made in the workplace is endless, and will often depend on the nature of the role. Personalised suggestions can be made by an occupational health professional, frequent lateness means that they don't care about being on time, or that difficulty meeting deadlines means that they don't care about their work. This is rarely true, but it's common for people with ADHD to worry about how they are perceived by others.

Some employees with ADHD may have a talent for problem solving and an increased ability to 'think outside the box'. It's also common for people with ADHD to show high levels of creativity, and research actually shows that people with ADHD tend to be more creative than those who do not. One interesting study found that, within a group of college students, those with ADHD had a preference for coming up with new ways to solve problems,

"Employees with ADHD are good at thinking up new ideas"

while those without preferred to use existing methods. When applied to the workplace, this could mean that employees with ADHD are strong innovators who are good at thinking up new ideas and ways of working.

Often the key to thriving at work with ADHD is to find a position that fits with a person's skills and interests. Although a repetitive administrative job may not seem appealing, other professions like teaching, journalism, healthcare and catering provide work environments that are more dynamic. People with ADHD are often able to stay calm in crisis situations, and their ability to keep their emotions under control while managing difficult and high pressure situations can make them ideal candidates for jobs in the emergency services.

"Specific workplace coaching is also available for people who have ADHD"

So, what should someone with ADHD look for in a job? As well as finding work that fits with their skills and interests, people with ADHD may find it helpful to work in a role that provides a structured day, with plenty of stimulation and opportunity for movement. It could also be useful to be able to access regular and fairly immediate feedback, in a way that doesn't leave them feeling too constricted and micromanaged. For jobs that don't offer these things, it's often possible to request adaptations that will make the workplace more accessible, and in many countries providing reasonable adjustments is a legal right.

The list of potential adjustments that can be made in the workplace is endless, and will often depend on the nature of the role. Personalised suggestions can be made by an occupational health professional,

Supporting women

It's well known that men and women often experience different symptoms when it comes to ADHD, and this can impact the support that they receive in the workplace. While all genders may experience ADHD masking, this tends to be more prevalent in women, and can result in women using masking behaviours to hide their ADHD traits at work.

Examples of how this can manifest includes working late to compensate for inattentiveness during the working day, or calling in sick rather than risk turning up late. Women may also nod or pretend to take notes after zoning out during a meeting, and then panic after realising that they didn't manage to absorb important information.

Ultimately, instead of discussing their difficulties, women are more likely to hide them, and this often results in them not having their needs met. Over time this can lead to increased fatigue, decreased job performance and burnout. Unmasking can carry a risk, but employers can support neurodivergent women by providing a safe space to discuss their challenges and potential supportive adaptations. Employers should also be aware that it is much more likely for adult women to remain undiagnosed, and offer support with screening and diagnosis.

who will be aware of an individual's difficulties and how changes may be implemented. For example, a 15-minute flexibility window for someone who struggles to arrive to work on time, may ease any pressure associated with punctuality. If it feels helpful, employees with ADHD may appreciate receiving increased supervision or regular planning meetings, where they can work together on developing and maintaining checklists and reminder systems. It could also be very useful for instructions to be received written instead of verbally, in order to help with their memory and also their prioritisation.

For those who work in open-plan offices, noise-cancelling headphones can be a simple adaptation that effectively reduces distractions and increases focus. Regular movement breaks can also be a very helpful way to manage hyperactivity and distractibility, whether that's for a short walk around the office or outside to get a breath of fresh air.

As well as working closely with their line manager and the occupational health department,